THE GREAT GREAT AUNTS FROM PRUSSIA

A HISTORICAL ROMANCE NOVEL
WRITTEN BY

ROBERT BECKSTEDT

Copyright © 2025 Robert Beckstedt.

All rights reserved. No part of this publication may be reproduced, distributed, or transmitted in any form or by any means, including photocopying, recording, or other electronic or mechanical method, without the prior written permission of the publisher, except in the case of brief quotations embodied in critical reviews and certain other noncommercial uses permitted by copyright law.

This book is a work of fiction. All names, characters, locations, and incidents are products of the author's imaginations. Any resemblance to actual persons, things, living or dead, locales, or events is entirely coincidental.

ISBN: 979-8-89419-686-2 (sc)
ISBN: 979-8-89419-687-9 (hc)
ISBN: 979-8-89419-688-6 (e)

Because of the dynamic nature of the Internet, any web addresses or links contained in this book may have changed since publication and may no longer be valid. The views expressed in this work are solely those of the author and do not necessarily reflect the views of the publisher, and the publisher hereby disclaims any responsibility for them.

Technical support: Katharine Randall
Proofreader : Christopher Hepp

One Galleria Blvd., Suite 1900, Metairie, LA 70001
(504) 702-6708

Other Novels Written by Robert Beckstedt

Ian and Anton

I Murdered Your Mother, I think?

The Tributaries of Alex Beckham

Inspirations

"Of two sisters
one is always the watcher,
one the dancer."
**—Louise Glück,
<u>Descending Figure</u>**

"Words don't have the power to hurt you, unless that person meant
more to you than you are willing to confess."
—Shannon L. Alder

"You only live once, but if you do it right, once is enough."
—Mae West

"You've gotta dance like there's nobody watching,
Love like you'll never be hurt,
Sing like there's nobody listening,
And live like it's heaven on earth."
—William W. Purkey

Dedication

I wish to dedicate this novel to previous generations who followed the path of love for family and self-respect for themselves. As each generation and its members teach the next, I am grateful for those influences and my pride in those now going forward.

Author's Note

People ask if my novels are fiction or non-fiction. My first writing professor taught me two things about fiction. First, as soon as you write something in the third person and tell a reader what the character is thinking, it is fiction.

Secondly, if one writes fiction, it must be true. Not the story line, but the timeline, historical dates, technology of the time, and one's internal interpretation of the theme, 'To thine own self be true.'

The Great Great Aunts from Prussia began with my ten-year-old grandson Declan. On the release of my first novel, *I Murdered your Mother, I think?* in 2018, he approached me. 'Grandpa, can I read your book?' I smiled and told him, not yet. He responded, "When will you write a book I can read?" I then began my second, *The Tributaries of Alex Beckham*, a collection of short fun embellishments of my early years, age three to sixteen, 1953 to 1965. Its purpose was to give my future generations perspective as to their ancestors and the times in which we lived.

As I began the loosely related chapters of *The Tributaries of Alex Beckham* in short story fashion, I came to my relationship with my two elderly aunts. They were in their seventies, lived together their entire lives, and never married. The social term of the day was 'old maids' (and our favorite card game). They babysat me from infancy through my early school days. But as I initiated the chapter, I realized I had no idea who the family of Mayme and Carrie Wehmeyer were as they related to me.

I subscribed to Ancestry.com, researched the tree, and traced them back to the Prussian Empire. My aunts were born shortly after the Austro-Prussian War in 1866. My love of history grabbed hold. I went to Wikipedia and researched the times, and in particular, the Austro-Prussian War. It was interesting but nothing profound. I was about to leave the page and return to the events of 1956, but something happened. At the very end of the Wikipedia page, one line remained. It read,

"At the Battle of Langensalza, Red Cross nurses were allowed on a battlefield for the first time in history."

There was the story. It grew exponentially in my head. The story time-traveled over a century, back and forth, twists and turns, historical facts, and, guess who my great-great gandmother became? She was Maria Rothert, the first Red Cross Head Nurse ever on a battlefield.

Well, that part is fiction but, what was to be a short, and somewhat mundane chapter in *The Tributaries of Alex Beckham,* changed to a fun, stand-alone, novella.

If you are a fellow writer, or want to be, consider the infinitesimal amount of information available. If you have a story but you think it too simple, rummage through the endless piles of digital data until you find a seed, then plant it. The research is as fun as the story.

I hope you enjoy reading this novella as such as I enjoyed writing it.

Robert Beckstedt

1

The Home of Mayme and Carrie Wehmeyer

Cincinnati, Ohio
The Summer of 1956

The dog days of summer lay heavy on the city. Even the nights granted no relief from the heat. The sisters shared a double mattress in their one-bedroom home. The sheets were damp with their unwelcome perspiration. Each consistently rotated their pillows to provide some similitude of coolness to their cheeks; constant sleep was impossible. An oscillating fan in front of the window caused a slight breeze, moving humid air throughout the bedroom; occasionally it drifted across their bodies. Their saggy brassieres and panties played a useless role in combating their discomfort.

As daybreak touched softly on the walls, the phone rang loudly from the music room in the front of the house. As Mayme continued to snore, Carrie grabbed her cotton robe and painfully shuffled to answer the phone. As she turned on the light, she lost her balance causing one hand to crash upon the keyboard. The beautiful Baldwin upright was provoked into a thunderclap of chaotic sharps and flats.

In a voice coated with nighttime gruff, she answered, "Uh, good morning. Who may I ask is calling?"

"Mayme, this is Mary."

"No Mary, this is Carrie. Is everything all right, honey?" Carrie was scared something happened to her nephew, Alex. She was lovingly overprotective of him.

"Everything is fine. I'm sorry to wake you this early. I know this is short notice, but one of the girls went into labor last night, and they need me to cover for her. Can you watch Alex for the next two weeks?" Mary was apologetic yet knew Alex's Aunt Mayme and Aunt Carrie loved to take care of their little five-year-old. He was the love of their lives.

"Mary, yes, of course. When will you drop him off?"

"Ten minutes? Randall and I are leaving the house right now. Is that a problem?"

Carrie was fine with the time, but she felt uncomfortable exposing herself to Alex in her present attire; Mayme was still asleep.

"You have a key to our front door; let yourself in and take him to the living room. I need a few minutes to get dressed, then I'll feed him breakfast. I love cooking for that little boy, and he loves my pancakes."

"Carrie, he had cereal and…"

"Nonsense Mary, that skinny little thing eats like a horse. I assure you; he will never pass up my pancakes. And we made a fresh batch of anise cookies."

"Did you make them strong with a lot of what you Germans call Anise wine? We call it Sambuca, Carrie, and they can be too strong for Alex." Mary trusted Carrie to tell her the truth, but Mayme, not so much. Mayme was not shy when it came to her daily allotment of Sambuca.

"No, Mary, I made this batch myself. Be sure to bring his swimsuit. We'll take him to the kiddie pool down the street this afternoon; it's going to be a hot one." Carrie had no intention of swimming with

Alex. Her job was to watch over Alex and Mayme and keep them safe. Her sister Mayme was unique. She loved Alex, and their relationship was one of playmates. It was never more evident than in the kiddie-pool. Mayme never misses a chance to start a water fight with Alex and the other kids. They loved to hear her giggle.

"He has his swimsuit. I'll tell him to wait for you in the living room. Carrie, thank you so much. I will pick him up at five o'clock. See you soon."

Mary hung up and ran to the car. Randall and Alex were packed and ready to go.

"Come on, Mary, we are both late as it is." Randall backed out of the driveway. "To Mayme and Carrie's?"

"Yes, they can keep him all day."

"They love keeping him; Carrie I trust, Mayme, well…"

Alex interrupted from the backseat. "Aunt Mayme is kinda different Dad, but she is so much fun. She plays with me the most. Aunt Carrie just takes care of me; she feeds me and makes me take a bath and stuff. But Aunt Mayme gives me horsey rides, wrestles with me on the floor, and plays with me in the pool. She even tries to run through the sprinkler, but she doesn't do it very well. She's like playing with my friends, only funnier." Alex was always excited to stay with his aunts.

Randall glanced at Mary from the corner of his eye. Mary knew what Randall was thinking; they discussed it. Randall's concern was Mayme's childlike behavior at seventy-six. He never thought she would purposely put him in any danger. Their concerns were addressed with Carrie. She promised never to leave the two alone; she never shared that promise with Mayme.

Randall parked in front of the Wehmeyer home. "Take him in and no chatting. You know how Mayme likes to talk, and I know how you like to talk. Remember, we are running late."

"I get it, Randall." Mary rolled her eyes. She took Alex into the house and directly to the living room. Carrie was in the bathroom making herself presentable. Mayme came out of the bedroom. She asked Mary questions relevant to nothing. "Mayme, I must run. I am already late for work. Let's visit when I pick Alex up at five."

"Alex is here?" Mayme smiled ear to ear; now even she considered her questions irrelevant. "Good, Carrie can take us to the pool today." She was bubbling with excitement. She followed Mary to the door.

"Mayme, my dear, see you tonight." Randall was surprised Mary came out so quickly. She did keep it short. Mayme followed her onto the porch in her brassiere and panties. She waved to Randall; Mary hopped into the car.

"Mayme looks a bit scary in the morning, especially in lingerie and no teeth," said Randall with a smirk.

"Be nice, Randall, you will look like that soon enough. You'll be bald, fat, and ugly, but I will still be cute." Mary returned the smirk.

Randall leaned over and kissed her on the cheek. "They are two sweet old maids. We are lucky to have somebody who loves our son so much. I'll pick up a bottle of Sambuca so they can make more cookies." They laughed at the irony. Mary and Randall waved and sped off to work.

2

Alex Beckham's Ancestry is Launched Heroically into the Past

Alex sat quietly on the time-worn sofa; his hands crossed on his lap. He was not a morning person, but even looking tired, he was adorable. He was skinny but healthy; in his swimsuit one could count all his ribs. He had a blonde burr haircut which pronounced his peanut-shaped head. His teeth were both bucked and gaped, but his smile and naïve intelligence were so lovable. Carrie dressed in the bathroom, combed her thinning white hair with her pearl-handled brush; she inserted her false teeth from the glass. Alex knew Carrie needed time to get ready, but it was obvious Mayme was not concerned about her appearance. She felt no need to delay seeing her precious Alex. Her deep obsession with him was a mystery to Mary and Randall, but not to Carrie.

"How is my little brother this morning?" For a moment, Alex was puzzled. She sat next to him on the couch and gave him a hug, then a tender kiss on his cheek. "We're going to have some fun today. Let's go to the pool this afternoon and maybe play in the sprinkler this morning."

Alex's feelings were mixed. He never saw his Aunt Mayme this early in the morning. Her hair was wet from the night's perspiration;

it created an unpleasant odor. She was without teeth. He was unsure whether to laugh at the way she talked or be disturbed by the way she looked; or both. Alex was taught to be respectful. He gave her a reciprocal hug, but he really did not want to, at least not until she put on some clothes, cleaned up, and put in her teeth.

"Mom told me to tell you we are sorry for getting you out of bed so early."

"Not at all, Alex, your Aunt Carrie will cook you breakfast while I go back to sleep for a while. I know how much you love her pancakes; I do too. And after you eat breakfast, you can nap on the couch if you wish. It's early for you too, honey." Mayme yawned, stretched her arms, and began her trek back to her bedroom, via the kitchen. She disappeared into the pantry.

"Did you make cookies last night, Aunt Mayme? Can I have some for breakfast?"

Mayme yelled from the pantry, "Uh, well, yes, we do have fresh anise cookies, and you can have as many as you like. We make them mostly for you, your grandpa, and Francis."

"Who is Francis, Aunt Mayme?"

Mayme did not respond. She came out of the pantry attempting to hide a bottle of Sambuca behind her back and a shot glass in one hand. She returned to her room and sat on the edge of her bed. She downed two shots of the sweet liqueur, then reclined peacefully. The Sambuca gently removed the aches and pains in her arthritic joints. She fell asleep within minutes, snoring so loudly Alex heard her in the living room. He was giggling when Carrie walked into the room. She smiled and snorted like a pig to mock her sister; they both snickered like school children.

"Come, my child, I will make you breakfast." Alex rose from the sofa and followed Carrie like a kitten who heard a can opener. Carrie prepared her nephew his favorite. "I think I have everything you need, milk, butter, and syrup. Can you think of anything else?"

"The pancakes look perfect, Aunt Carrie. Mom burns them most of the time." Carrie loved to make her little nephew happy. She had no children of her own, only nieces and nephews. To take care of them was the most joyous task in her life. She poured herself a cup of coffee and joined Alex at the table.

"Aunt Carrie, I have a question I keep meaning to ask my mom, but then I forget." Carrie was having trouble understanding Alex with his cheeks packed with pancakes like a baby squirrel.

"Alex, don't talk with your mouth full. Take your time and chew your food." Carrie waited patiently; she had no clue what Alex might ask. She knew her great-great-nephew was inquisitive and thought it would be about Mayme's Sambuca bottle.

He swallowed, but with a bite still on his fork pointed at the ceiling, he asked, "I sometimes hear you and Aunt Mayme and Grandpa talk to each other in words I never heard before. I hear people talk that way on Grandpa's huge radio in his hallway. I think my brain might be going weird. Is it?"

Carrie laughed; she stroked the soft bristles on Alex's head. "Oh honey, not at all. Your brain's not weird. We are talking in a language called German. That's the language my parents spoke when they lived in Prussia. Then they taught Mayme and me when we were growing up in Boston."

Alex still was unclear why they spoke German. "Why do you speak that German language now when you live here? People can't understand you, you know."

Carrie smiled once more at Alex's innocence. "Germany is where your great-great grandparents were born, only it was called Prussia back then."

"Wait, who were they again? That who was related to who thing always messes me up."

"Okay, let me explain. Your Grandpa Schaefer's grandparents, the people he called 'Grandma and Grandpa,' were August and Maria

Wehmeyer; that is my last name. They were born over a hundred years ago in Prussia. There was Mayme and me, my mother and father, and we had six other brothers and sisters." Carrie thought that might make more sense to this young mind but, by the look on Alex's face, Carrie lost him right from the start.

"You mean Russia, Aunt Carrie. I've never heard of Prussia, but I have heard of Russia. They're the people who want to drop bombs on us and blow us up, right?"

"That's true, sort of, but Prussia was a country in Europe for a long time. Then there was a war, and Prussia took over a lot of little countries. Then they changed their name to Germany. In fact, your great-great-grandparents are in the history books. My father was a war hero, and my mother was one of the first Red Cross nurses ever on a battlefield. They were famous, and well-respected." Carrie was proud of her heritage and excited to share it with Alex. She knew he was an intelligent child, and he just might be old enough to enjoy the story.

"Really? I have a grandpa who was famous?"

"Yes, and a grandmother."

"I want to hear more, but since it happened way back in Russia, I mean Prussia, can you tell me in English? I don't understand German." Alex was ready. He loved stories. He thought *I hoped this story is as fun as the stories Dad reads me about those history and bible people.*

"Alex, I can't tell you the whole story at once. It is long. But since you will be staying here for a couple of weeks, I will tell you a little at a time while Mayme sleeps. How does that sound?"

"Sounds great, Aunt Carrie. Can you write down some notes so I can write a book about it someday? I am still a year away from learning how to read and write."

"Yes, I took notes over the years. I will tell you what my mother and father told me. But before we start, let me check on Aunt Mayme." Carrie entered the room quietly; she whispered, "Are you okay,

Mayme?" A loud snort confirmed she was asleep. She placed her hand gently on Mayme's head and smiled. She was excited to begin the story of her mother and father in Prussia. And Alex was just as excited to hear it.

3

Private August Wehmeyer Returns from The Battle of Langensalza

Wehmeyer Garden
Berlin, Prussia
September 15, 1866

"Alright, Alex, let's begin. My father met my mother on a battlefield in Prussia. He was a soldier in the Battle of Langensalza in 1866, during which he was shot through the shoulder, knocked out by the butt of a pistol, and blinded by an exploding cannon shell."

"And he didn't die? Wow!"

"No, somehow he did not, but my mother, a nurse in the newly formed Red Cross, found him and returned him to the camp to be treated."

"Where is Langensalza, and your father was a soldier?"

"Yes, but let me continue. Strangely enough, my mother and father became friends right away. They exchanged addresses. My father was sent home and when the war ended, my mother wrote to him every week."

"So, that is how they got married?"

"Well, not quite. Since he was blind, his twin sister read her letters to him, but he was scared one of her letters would be her last."

"Was one, Aunt Carrie? Was one her last?"

"No more questions, dear boy. Let me begin. It starts with my father and his younger brother in the garden of their home in Berlin, the capital of Prussia."

———∞∞∞———

"Aww, kissy, kissy, another letter from your little sweetie, eh August? I bet she writes ten of those a day to all the other boys she met in Langensalza." August could see the faint shadow of his brother through the bandages that protected his decimated eyes. But with the loss of one sense, his hearing became more astute to what moved around him. Playfully, Henry slapped August on the back, then ran around him like a neurotic puppy. As Henry teased his big brother with another slap, he was not accepting the fact they were not little boys any longer. August prepared to attack. Seeing Henry's shadow, August grabbed him like a snake striking a field mouse. Life had grown around these brothers like weeds in an unkept plot of land. August was not the innocent, loving lad he was before he joined the Prussian army three years prior. He fought brutally against the Danes in the Second Schleswig War, then the Hanoverians in the Austro-Prussian War.

Unlike August's gentle nature in the past, August had the front of his brother's white school shirt in a violent grip. He pulled Henry into his face with a vicious, but unseen stare. And though Henry could not see August's eyes through the bandages, he could see his jaw clenched tightly with impatience. Henry was scared; tears filled the innocent boy's eyes. He was speechless as August's nostrils flared; his breathing was that of a madman.

"I warned you twice, you little asshole, and there will be no more warnings. Got it, Henry?" Their mother, Hilda, watched her two sons in the courtyard from the kitchen window. She came running, stunned to see her son of twenty-two handling his brother with such brutality.

"August, what are you doing? That is your little brother. You have never treated him like that; shame on you. You are a grown man August Wehmeyer, not a child. Let him go right now." With that, August pushed Henry onto the ground. He skidded on his behind, leaving a heavy grass stain and a rip in his woolen knickers.

"I'm warning you, Mother, just like I am warning Henry. My shoulder is in terrible pain, and those pills I have been taking for months are not helping. I cannot see, and I don't know if I ever will. He hits my shoulder one more time, and I'll knock him on his butt again."

Hilda was shocked by this unexpected outrage of her oldest son; by far the most mature of her six children. But now she understood.

"Henry, you slapped your brother on his wounded shoulder. Is that why he is angry with you? My goodness, son, your brother had a bullet go through him from front to back only three months ago. What were you thinking? You strike your brother again, and I promise you, your father will take care of you in the shed. You will be unable to sit for a long, long time." She was overwhelmed with happiness when August returned. He survived numerous battles, but like any mother, she was bereaved by his blindness. And she sensed his anger was something more than his sight and his shoulder. Something else happened in Langensalza, and it had to do with the letters he received every week.

"Henry, go in the house; I want to speak with August alone." Henry, weeping from his brother's violent reaction and severe scolding from his mother, got up off the lawn and ran inside. To Henry, August was always his hero. But now, Henry feared those days were over. "It is not just your shoulder, is it August? You have been different since you returned from Langensalza. Do you want to talk about it? Is it those letters that trouble you so much?"

"NO!" August yelled; his nostrils flared once again. "I do not want to talk about it, and that little twit torments me every time I get a letter from her. I am telling you, Mother, I never want to think or talk about that battlefield ever again. She is the only one who knows what happened that godawful day, and it shall remain that way. So, if any of you wish to bring it up, I will not stand for it."

"August, it must have been something terrible if you are this upset. We all love you, honey. So, this girl was with you in Langensalza?" His mother's heart was breaking.

"It was war, Mother. No one gets over it, so stop; just stop it." August refused to be coddled and was in no mood to be interrogated. "And who told you the letters are from a girl? It had to be Katerina."

"We just assumed it was from a girl, but you confirmed it when you said Henry torments you when you get a letter from her."

"Okay, it's a girl."

"What can I do to help, my love? May I ask, what kind of friend is she? Your father and I are curious. When did you find time to meet a girl when you were in ranks the whole time?"

"I said leave it alone, Mother." It was unusual for August to be indignant with her, but she wouldn't stop. "It is none of your business. If I choose to have a private life, then…"

"You are correct. I have no right to interfere; I am sorry. I just love you and want to help." Hilda walked back to the kitchen; her eyes welling with tears. August could not see them, but he could hear her faint whimper.

———⁕⁕⁕———

"Alex, we must stop for today. I just saw Marme heading to the bathroom. I will tell you more tomorrow."

"Sounds like your father was kinda mean the way he treated his mom and brother. Was he mean to you, too?"

"Not at all, Alex. He was the kindest and bravest man I ever knew. You wouldn't be too happy if you were shot through the shoulder and blinded by a cannon shell. He was trying to figure out what to do with his life. He was scared he would be the man sitting on a corner, begging for money with a tin cup. And he was still in a lot of pain."

"So, what did he do?"

"Remember, a little at a time. I will continue tomorrow. Let's get ready for the pool."

4

Prussian Families Prepare for War Five Days Before The Battle of Langensalza

Cologne, Prussia
June 22, 1866
Friday

It was another hot summer day. Alex and Carrie had breakfast. Mayme was asleep. Alex was anxious to hear more. "You haven't said much about your mother. How did she become a nurse on a battlefield? And you said something about a Red Cross. Does it have something to do with Sunday School?"

Carrie smiled. "No, nothing to do with Sunday School; and it is The Red Cross, not a Red Cross. Let me tell you it and about her. She was only eighteen when she went to war. She was a brave young woman, as brave as my father. It was a strange series of events which brought them together."

"Tell me about her. Now she was my what?"

"Great-great-grandmother, and that is why I am your great-great aunt."

"I'll figure all that out someday. But now, tell me about your mother. I want to hear about her, Aunt Carrie." Carrie smiled again.

Joseph and Ida Rothert sat impatiently at the massive dining room table adorned with a white heirloom tablecloth. The silence was broken as their daughter entered the room. "Maria Rothert, where have you been? You know we eat dinner at five o'clock sharp. You are one hour late." Maria scolded her; Joseph sat quietly. Joseph's coffee steamed in front of him; his spoon clanked on his china cup as he stirred in a second sugar cube. When the swirling came to rest, he saw his own frowning reflection. Ida stared intensely at her daughter; the interrogation began.

"I had something I had to do, Mother, and it could not wait." Joseph sat quietly. Maria's four brothers and two sisters had been excused from the table and went outside to play; their chairs neatly positioned back under the table.

"Little girl, just because you graduated from High School last week does not give you the privilege of keeping your father and your siblings waiting. I am sorry, but you will only receive cold scraps, if any remain. They are in the kitchen. Anna might be so kind as to fix you a plate if she has not finished with the dishes. Her workday is complete when they are clean." Ida's scolding was taken with no fear. But if Joseph needed to become involved, whippings with a switch were possible.

Joseph gently blew on his steaming coffee as he held the cup to his lips. "Daughter, ask Anna to prepare a plate for you, then return as she performs this undeserved task. Being tardy for dinner is unacceptable in this family, no matter how old you may be." Joseph was calm, but Maria knew his demeanor was not one of acceptance.

"Yes, Father." Maria knew what she was about to tell her parents was to be either a proud moment for all or one to cause a clash in their relationship.

Maria was raised in an intellectual and sophisticated environment. Her father was a well-respected physician in the city of Cologne. He adapted the west wing of his inherited family mansion into three exam rooms and a small operatory. He treated many people of the urban population and the surrounding farmlands.

Although most of his practice consisted of routine illness and minor injuries, four years prior, Joseph witnessed three horrific battles in the American Civil War. Otto Von Bismarck insisted Prussian surgeons learn from the American field doctors as he prepared for the imminent Austro-Prussian War. Von Bismarck and King Wilhelm I wished to unite the Germanic-speaking provinces, but not through diplomacy.

Joseph spoke little of his journey except to teach his colleagues surgical and amputation skills. His family was proud of his bravery, but when he returned in 1863, his temperament changed from gentle to intolerant. What he experienced on the battlefields left him unable to relate to the social elites. His presence within the upper circles of Cologne diminished rapidly.

Maria reentered the formal dining room and sat in her assigned seat, one chair to the left of her father; her mother sat at the other end. "Father, I am sorry I am late for dinner, but I heard something and my immediate attention to the situation was mandatory." Maria sat with her hands folded in her lap, expressing her ladylike posture to perfection.

Ida still did not approve of this break in tradition. "Look at me, young one. What could be so important that this crucial task could not wait until Monday? Your school days are over until you attend the university in the fall. Our family is strong because we respect each other's time, and we meet to give thanks to the Lord every evening as one."

Maria began to speak, her voice trembled in anticipation of the unknown reaction from her parents, especially her father. "Father, I wish to apologize to you and Mother. I understand and respect our family traditions to the highest but allow me to explain." Joseph was impressed with the social skills and rhetoric of his oldest daughter.

"Please, and I hope for your sake there are no falsifications in your story," Joseph responded.

"No sir, those days of my youth are behind me. Allow me to begin by saying, this past week of Bible study with Pastor Braun has been enlightening, and today an event occurred which caused me to act upon his teachings." Although trembling, Maria was speaking in a most mature manner.

Ida interjected sternly. "Keep going, Maria, but there best be a sound reason why you are using a man of the cloth to excuse your tardiness."

"Get on with it, child." Joseph was becoming impatient.

"Pastor Braun also teaches a class in our Lutheran High School. He teaches current events."

"Yes, and what does…?" interrupted Ida.

"Ida, let the girl speak. I am interested in why the pastor is involved in educating our children as to the situations in our world. He should be teaching of the world beyond." Joseph was skeptical as to any clergy sharing opinions on politics.

Maria began again. "Thank you, Father. As I was saying, the pastor teaches us what is happening in our current political environment. He told us two years ago, in 1864, an organization was founded in Geneva to help soldiers injured in battle, like you did in America."

"Yes, Maria, I am aware of the organization. It is called the Red Cross and is chartered by the First Geneva Convention. Our country signed the agreement and joined this international group. It protects those who display red crosses on their arms, dresses, and shirts. However, they may only help soldiers of their own country." Since his experience in America, Joseph became close to the powerful Otto Von Bismarck. Prussian government officials were instructed to consult with Joseph regarding training manuals for the nurses and medics of the Red Cross. He was a key figure in its startup, unbeknownst to his family.

"So, what does this have to do with being late for dinner, child?" Ida snapped once more.

"My friends and I graduated from High School last Friday and are eighteen years of age."

"Yes, we know that. Go on," Ida snipped.

"Well, the pastor's son, Otto, and five other boys from my class were served draft notices on Monday, three days after our graduation. I learned today they must leave for somewhere this Monday. Rumors are they are going to war." Maria's eyes began to moisten.

"Oh my, that is terrible. Those boys are far too young to go into the army. What is wrong with Von Bismarck? He cannot take our children from us. For God's sake, they have been out of school less than a week. Tomorrow, Joseph, I insist we go to the induction center and protest. Otto Braun is like one of our own. He and Maria spent hours in this house together." Ida was shocked. "So, Maria, you were late because you were saying goodbye to Otto? That is precious, and we certainly forgive you."

"No Mother, he is gone. He had to report yesterday. When I heard, I went to Otto's home on Wednesday, and we talked."

Joseph sat quietly. He was putting the puzzle pieces together; he was fearful he was right. "Then why were you late? You are not making sense, child." Ida was again losing her patience.

"Say it, Maria; just say it. You were late because you joined the Red Cross. Am I correct?"

"Yes sir," Maria answered as she looked proudly into her father's eyes.

"No, no, no," said Ida. "I forbid it. You are too young, and you have no training to help them. War means injury and death for anyone close to it. If you are not injured physically, you will be mentally. Look at your father. Since he returned …"

Ida was interrupted. "Ida, don't say it. I know I am not the same person since I returned from America, but the Lord needs my help. That is why I became a physician and trained to be a surgeon. How can we blame our daughter for following in the footsteps of her father? I am the one at fault." Joseph sighed as his mind stared into a scene he never imagined.

"No, Joseph, that is different. You are a strong man. You are a smart man. And even though you are not the same since you returned, your skills will save many. What can this child do on a field of battle? She knows nothing."

"Ida, that is not true. She helped me many times when patients came to visit. She assisted me in stitching. She assisted me in cleaning wounds; and she bandaged many of my patients; she has a natural talent for it." Maria did not expect that response from her father. However, she decided she would be a volunteer for the Red Cross no matter what her parents said.

"No, I will go down tomorrow morning and insist she not be allowed to volunteer in such a dangerous endeavor. Joseph, she is a child."

"Mother, I am eighteen and please stop calling me a child. I am capable of choosing my own future. You have no authority to force them to refuse me. I do not need your permission." Ida was now furious; Joseph intervened.

"Ida, I know you are terrified you will lose your little girl, but she is not a little girl any longer. She is a young woman, and a brave one. As frightened as I am for her to be in harm's way, and the brutality of soldiers and their unspeakable acts towards women in these situations, I am proud of her." Maria saw a gentle smile on her father's face along with tears welling in his eyes.

"Thank you, Father." Maria held her head high and observed the expressions on her parents' faces.

The Great Great Aunts from Prussia

Ida buried her head in her arms on the table and wept. As she did, Joseph spoke to Maria. "My daughter, I must warn you of a danger you may not have considered."

"Yes, Father, what is it? All I know right now is I am going with my friends who were drafted into the Prussian Army as a Red Cross nurse. I will treat the wounded and help save lives as I have watched my father do. I have proofread your government manuals for you many times. I am ready."

"No Maria, that is not it. You realize the Red Cross has never been in a battle? This will be the first time their volunteers will be permitted on a battlefield. Prussia and many other nations pledged their support for the rules of the organization, and those countries will train their soldiers to protect you from both sides."

"Yes, I know, Father. I read the entire enactment after Pastor Braun made me aware. So, what do I not know?"

"Prussia signed the agreement, but Austria and its allies did not. If you are shot by an Austrian soldier, it will not be considered a war crime; just part of the battle." Ida raised her head with terror in her eyes.

"Father, what makes you think they won't sign it before war breaks out? That may be a year. I could still be in training. They have forty-three volunteers already. They won't send us into battle without training, would they?"

"You told them you worked with me, correct?"

"Yes."

"Then you are experienced as far as the Red Cross is concerned. And about a war not coming for a year, they would not be drafting all these young men and sending them away this quickly if a war were not coming soon. I suspect by the end of next week. Troops are moving into Langensalza as we speak, and that includes Otto and your friends."

"How do you know that, Joseph?" asked Ida with deep curiosity.

"Ida, I was going to tell you after dinner, but I must tell you now. I received a visit from an army captain today. He had a telegram from

Von Bismarck asking me to join and coordinate the Red Cross team. Maria and I will both leave Monday for Langensalza on the train with both soldiers and medical personnel."

"No Joseph, why must you go too? Why must you both leave so soon?"

"Ida, Von Bismarck did not send me to America to sightsee. He told me, if Prussia went to war, my services would be needed. No, the term he used was 'mandatory'." Silence came over the table.

Ida broke down crying once again. She knew she may not only lose her daughter, but her husband as well. Maria and Joseph got up from their chairs and went to Ida. They hugged her and her terrified soul.

"Ida, we will be fine. We have God's work to do. Be proud of us and pray for us every night. We will return soon."

Then Joseph hugged Maria with an embrace she had never felt. It was one of mature love and respect. "We will be on the same train and in the same car together with other medical providers. I will help with your training and the training of others on our way. You have proofread my manuals several times. I will need your help as much as you will need mine."

"I love you, Father." Maria returned the hug.

"I love you too, my dear. Now, let us prepare to save some brave soldiers. You are about to make history, Maria Rothert. You will be among the first Red Cross nurses on a battlefield. It will be a proud day for our family and for generations to come."

"Wow, so she joined that Red Cross thing all by herself. Then what?"

"Well Alex, I think we have time before Mayme wakes. Let me tell you some more."

"Be back in a minute, Aunt Carrie." Alex scampered off to the bathroom.

5

*The Train from Cologne to Langensalza
Leaves in Forty-Eight Hours
No Time to Rest -- No Time for Fear*

Cologne, Prussia
June 23/24, 1866
Sat./Sun.

Joseph began the day by giving Maria the title of Head Nurse. They spent the rest of the day expanding Maria's medical skills so she could prepare her nurses for the battlefield. After the final updates to Joseph's training manual, Maria delivered it to the printer to be ready by Sunday evening. Day one was complete.

Maria slept lightly, so lightly she floated poetically through an ethereal part of her mind, reviewing the events which delivered her to this critical juncture of her life. She mentally leafed through the pages of her childhood: her teachers, pastor, friends, family. She realized her decision to go to war so young was not an emotional impulse. Every path on which her twilight thoughts led her made her realize her life progressed as destined. She seemed to be walking down a narrow passageway, unable to exit until the end where dawn filled the sky. She peered into the wide-open space. The sun rose over grassy knolls which seemed to roll endlessly. Her mind pondered, *what awaits me in the valley below each mysterious hilltop?*

"Maria, are you awake?" her father whispered in her ear; he nudged her and kissed her softly on the cheek. Joseph did not want to wake Maria's younger sister; the sister who she shared a room with for ten years.

"Yes, Father, I'm awake. Is something wrong?" Maria sat up and rubbed her eyes. The early morning sunlight crept through the small-paned window.

"All is well, my dear. It is time to prepare for our departure. We leave tomorrow morning, so we must gather our supplies and instruments today. We have no time to spare. I would like for us to enjoy dinner as a family tonight before we leave." Joseph was careful not to use the phrase "one last time," and he no longer viewed his daughter as a child. He would be unable to treat her as one for the rest of her life, and she would give him no reason to do so.

"Father, give me a moment to brush my teeth, cleanse my face, and dress. I will join you for breakfast. I reviewed what you taught me all night, but I want to learn more, and quickly." Joseph gently caressed Maria's hair with a look of pride on his face. Overnight she exploded into adulthood like a thunderbolt. He knew this was the end of her innocence, as it was for him when he viewed the world's inhumanity in the American Civil War. Joseph knew he changed dramatically upon his return, and he knew Maria would never again view her family and friends as emotional peers. The sight of death and suffering destroys the fairytale world for anyone possessing a compassionate heart.

Maria came down the stairs; she pushed open the swinging door to the kitchen. Anna had breakfast spread neatly across the worn wooden table. The celestial aroma of her homemade loaves blanketed the room like an invisible cloud. The making of jam from blackberries grown in the garden was a cherished event between Maria and Anna. It brought smiles to their faces, but not this morning. All in the room knew the worst-case scenario for this beautiful family.

With tears in the eyes of Ida and Anna, they moved perpetually around the kitchen. Joseph and Maria sat across from each other on the long benches. The other children had not yet awakened. "Maria, I will make a list of medical supplies needed. Take the list to the army headquarters; ask for Captain Heil. Accompany him and his men to gather what we need to treat the wounded." Joseph's orders to Maria were given with no emotion, the same way he spoke to any assistant.

"If there are any wounded, Joseph," Ida interjected, correcting her husband in a most curt fashion. Maria looked at her father to observe his reaction.

"Yes, dear. I am assuming there will be some sort of battle. But you are correct, there may not be." Joseph did not argue with Ida. He was just as worried about his daughter's safety as she was. But Ida was the one with two loved ones for whom to worry. Joseph was not worried about himself; neither was Maria.

Maria returned to the topic, "But Father, should not the Red Cross personnel know what is necessary?" Joseph knew his daughter had asked a logical question even though naïve.

"My dear, from this point forward, we must have no secrets between us."

"I agree, Father. But what are you saying?"

"I will be wearing a Prussian officer's uniform and be the leader of this Red Cross mission. The Red Cross has never been in a battle in all of history. They have no field experience, therefore no field leaders. I do. That is why I made you Head Nurse. You volunteered; there is no turning back. I must trust you completely; and you me."

"Yes Father, I understand, but can we continue to discuss the supplies? What might the quantities be which are needed? How can I know that?"

Ida turned towards Joseph for the answer all wanted to hear. His answer would determine the size of the battle and the amount of dead and wounded. It would reveal the magnitude of the incursion.

"That is unknown to me at this point, Maria. Just tell Captain Heil the quantities are dependent upon his estimated number of wounded. Use these formulas of calculation. The quantities will be dependent upon each one hundred men wounded in battle. Multiply each supply by how many hundred. Do you understand, Maria?" Joseph was precise.

"Yes sir, I understand. I will leave now and report back as soon as the job is completed." Maria was no longer the schoolchild at the dinner table the night before. Even her mother and Anna recognized this instant evolution.

"Wait a moment, I am not finished." Joseph wrote on the second page of parchment with his quill. He finished quickly and pushed the parchment across the table to Maria. "Also, tell him the instruments listed on this side of the page must be multiplied by the number of doctors capable of amputations. On the other side of the page, multiply those instruments by surgeons capable of removing musket balls and cannon shrapnel from the soldiers' tissues and inner organs." Maria felt ill from the thought but suppressed it. She hid it courageously from her father, as well as Ida and Anna. The amputations her father performed were predominantly in America, but a few were in the small operatory at the local hospital. Suddenly, unable to control herself, Ida vomited into the sink.

Thinking he would lighten the conversation, Joseph asked "Ida, are we expecting another child?" His attempt at humor was bluntly ignored.

"Come Maria, let us finish this discussion in my office. Grab my instructions and your tea, and pack us a handful of those wonderful anise cookies your mother and Anna made yesterday. Ladies, we love these cookies. They will be a recipe to be handed down for generations." Joseph smiled, kissed Ida on the back of her head as she leaned over the sink. He winked at Anna. Maria trotted behind her father to keep up with the focused Dr. Rothert. But before they could exit through the swinging door, they were stopped. The reality of Maria's decision finally overflowed in Ida's heart.

Ida cried out. She stomped her foot. "No, Joseph, she is not going with you. She is not ready for that kind of horror. I forbid it!" Ida lost her composure, panic set in. But the events taking place tomorrow morning were now absolute. She always accepted her sons may go to war someday, but she never imagined her daughter.

Joseph did not respond. Maria looked over her shoulder at her mother's anguish. She continued following her father's orders, knowing he was more than that now. He was her commanding officer, and their lives depended on each other. The feelings in Maria's heart were mixed, but the overriding thought which drove her was one of destiny. Something pushed her into this abyss. It felt right. She felt it must be God's calling.

Ida buried her face in Anna's bosom; they both sobbed; they're filled with maternal grief. "Your daughter is a strong young woman, Ida. She will be protected by her spirit, the love of her family, and by God." Anna's tears dripped upon the top of Ida's beautiful blonde hair.

The day of preparation flew by like a flock of migrating geese. Joseph boxed his personal supplies and packed his surgical instruments in protective gauze. He then sat at his desk and prepared an agenda for the one-day train ride to Langensalza; a journey which must be planned with efficiency. He had limited time to teach his volunteers the fundamentals of triage, pre-op, the operatory, and post-op; it was a lot. While Joseph prepared his agenda, Maria bustled through the streets of Cologne with a band of soldiers gathering the instruments and supplies necessary.

Her plan was well organized. She joined her father many times in the purchase of medical needs. The soldiers moved their wagons from pharmacy to pharmacy, gathering precisely what her father instructed her in the quantities determined by the captain's estimations. Her youth and inexperience as a leader were quickly overridden by her professionalism. "Yes, Ma'am" and "No, Ma'am" were immediately found to be the appropriate salutation for this young woman displaying such subliminal administrative skills.

Maria's competence came naturally. She was now introduced as the head nurse of the newly founded Red Cross team. The soldiers knew she and her father were responsible for the wounded in the upcoming Battle of Langensalza. But Maria thought nothing of the danger she would encounter, only the importance of the task at hand.

"Joseph," Ida shouted curtly as she stormed into his office; her arms folded and a scowl upon her face. "I told you dinner would be ready at five o'clock sharp; it is now thirty minutes past the hour. And where is Maria?" The other children were instructed to be silent as they sat with perfect posture at the table.

Joseph spoke, but did not look at Ida as he continued to pack his surgical instruments. "Ida, please, Maria will be home any time; I need ten more minutes. Please be understanding tonight, especially towards Maria. I do not believe you want to be angry tonight."

Ida was unable to control her ghastly visions of the days to come. Only forty-eight hours prior, Maria was scolded like a child for being late to dinner. Now, her husband and daughter no longer seemed part of the family, a family which, until yesterday, was organized and disciplined. "I will instruct Anna to begin serving the children. She prepared hasenpfeffer, mashed potatoes, green beans," she hesitated, "and sauerkraut. That is Maria's favorite. Ten minutes, Joseph, but if Maria is…"

Suddenly Maria, breathing heavily, burst into the room and interrupted her mother. "Sorry, Mother, Father, but I had to go to a few more stores in order to get the additional quantities the captain required."

Ida looked at Joseph. They both knew what the "additional quantities" meant, and from the tenseness in Maria's tone, she did as well. But the conversation was only acknowledged internally.

"What is that mouth-watering aroma, Mother? Is it Hasenpfeffer? Oh Mother, my favorite. Are we ready to eat? I have had nothing since breakfast." Maria was shaking slightly from the adrenaline pumping through her body.

"Yes Maria, dinner has been ready for a while, but you and your father have not. Joseph, come. You have all night to complete your preparations for tomorrow." With that, Joseph and Maria could see Ida's eyes change from impatience to tears. She turned and left the room.

"Father," Maria began, "I have a few things I must tell you, but nothing bad. I went to…"

Joseph interrupted. "Not now, Maria, your mother is right. The family has been waiting patiently for us, and dinner is late. We will talk after we eat." Joseph put his arm around her shoulder; they strolled into the dining room. They took their seats. Anna had dinner arranged beautifully on the table. The hasenpfeffer and its gravy smelled delectable.

"Oh Anna, you know that is my favorite. That is so sweet of you before Father and I…"

Joseph cleared his throat so Maria would not make this a sad occasion.

"It was your mother's idea, child. You and your father may not get a decent meal for weeks." Anna was being optimistic, but everyone knew it could be much longer, if ever, before Joseph and Maria returned.

Dinner progressed quietly. Nothing was said about dawn tomorrow. The children did not speak unless spoken to, and Ida only spoke to reprimand someone for an elbow on the table or to wipe one's mouth of an errant piece of food. As dinner ended, all the children, except Maria, were excused. As they left, one by one, they gave their oldest sister and their father a long and loving embrace. But Ida insisted no tears. Joseph, Ida, and Maria remained to finish their coffee.

Joseph looked at Ida. "Excuse us, my dear, but Maria must debrief me on the events of her day. Maria, use the bathroom if you must, then join me in my office." Ida sat alone at the table. She noticed how formal her husband was with Maria and how respectful Maria was to her father. They were both different.

"So, your mother's father was a doctor and worked for the King. And he could cut people's arms and legs off if he had to? Aunt Carrie, what is house in fuffer."

Carrie laughed. "Hasenpfeffer, Alex, it is pronounced Hasenpfeffer. It is stewed rabbit cooked in wine and vinegar; and a lot of onions."

"Yuk, really. They ate rabbits back in those days?"

"I still make it. Your grandpa loves it. Want to join us for dinner sometime?"

"No thank you. So, what is next? Does the war start?"

"Yes, tomorrow, my mother and her father leave for Langesalza where the war begins. Carrie looked at Alex. "I believe I heard the floor creak. Mayme is awake. Get your suit. Let's take Mayme swimming."

6

Playtime in the Park

The Home of the Wehmeyer Sisters
Cincinnati, Ohio
Summer of 1956

Mayme appeared in the dining room. "Did you have a good sleep, Aunt Mayme?" asked Alex with an elated smile on his face.

Mayme's eyes were bloodshot and blurry; she shuffled to the bathroom in her tattered flowery robe. "Be with you in a jiffy, my little cubby. Let your Aunt Mayme make herself look human. Carrie, can you make me some coffee along with toast and jam, the blackberry jam we jarred last fall?"

Mayme brushed her thin white hair and inserted her false teeth from the glass in the bathroom. Her teeth were loose. Many times, Alex watched them bounce across the floor after a spontaneous sneeze; it always caused him to giggle. While Mayme gathered herself, Carrie prepared a modest breakfast for her sister. Alex sat on the couch reviewing the history of his great grandparents in his head. Mayme, somewhat freshened, entered the dinette. Alex heard her and skipped to join her.

"Okay, it's time. Come here, my little pumpkin." Alex walked to his aunt who hugged him as tight as she could, but the affection in her heart was more than her ageing arms could express. Her odor was the same as Alex experienced around his grandparents; he found it the same around most old people. "We're going to the pool today, right? You brought your bathing suit, I pray. You are almost big enough to beat me in a water fight." Mayme stuck two fingers in her coffee cup and flicked it on Alex's face. "But not yet," she cackled.

Carrie wiped Alex's face with a napkin. "Mayme, behave, I mean it." Mayme continued to giggle like a little girl, "Go ahead, Alex, get her back. You have milk in front of you. Do it. She started it. It's okay."

"Aunt Carrie, I can't do that. If my mother ever found out…" Carrie interrupted and grabbed Alex by the hand. She stuck his fingers in his milk and forced Alex's to return the flip.

Mayme gave out with another haunting giggle, wiped her face, then made her way to Alex's chair. He knew what was coming. He tried to escape, but it was too late. She trapped him and began tickling; he laughed and squirmed. Alex loved his aunt and loved to play with her, but tickling was not fun. It was painful. Alex broke free and was about to run.

"Okay you two, that's enough. Mayme, finish your breakfast and both of you put on your bathing suits. Let's go swimming at the park. It is almost noon. Within the hour, all those little tadpoles from the neighborhood will swarm that place. Go on now, get ready."

Carrie remembered the days when Alex was a toddler when she watched Mayme wrestle with him on the floor. She remembered her chasing him around the house; Alex would laugh, and Mayme would snort like a monster. Carrie loved to put them down for a nap. She would pull up a chair and adore. She loved them both, especially together. Carrie aged gracefully. Putting on a bathing suit at seventy-five and splashing around in a kiddy pool was not her idea of fun, but it was for Mayme.

Alex came out of the bathroom. He wore his chlorine-faded bathing suit covered with seashells, and his white Mickey Mouse tee shirt; his grin was ear to ear. He bounced around like popcorn popping in the pot. "Hold still, little one." Carrie strapped his sandals to his unblemished feet. As she did, Mayme exited the bedroom in a swimsuit she must have worn in the roaring twenties. It resembled a navy-blue sailor's uniform, only with baggy feminine pants just below her knees. It had a sleeveless top and white mesh lace around her neck. But it was the pink bathing cap with a white flower protruding over one ear which tied it all together. She knew she was the most interesting woman in a kiddy pool, maybe ever.

"Aunt Mayme, how did you get those scars on your arms?"

Without hesitation, Carrie answered. "Alex, your Aunt Mayme used to grow roses; she was cut many times by their thorns."

Not hearing the question or the answer, Mayme blurted, "What are we waiting for? Let's go have some fun. Are you ready, polliwog? Hop on; I'll give you my famous horsey ride to the pool." Alex and Carrie glanced subtly at each other.

"Mayme, Alex is not as little as he used to be. I don't believe that is a good idea." Alex agreed and stayed silent, even though he missed those horsey-ride days. He especially missed the sound she made, more like a donkey's hee-haw, than the neighing of a horse.

"Nonsense Carrie, Art is only three. I gave him a ride just last week." Alex was confused whenever she called him by the name of his grandfather; Carrie was not. She understood why; it always caused a shiver of sadness inside her.

"Mayme, this is Alex, not Art, and he is not three, he is almost six. If you try to pick him up, you will hurt yourself." Carrie stayed close in case Mayme ignored her advice.

Mayme frowned and got closer to Alex's face. She looked at Carrie, then back at Alex. "You're not Art. Who are you, little boy? Art has a scar on his cheek. Tell me right now." Alex looked at Carrie, confused again by Mayme's inability to recognize him.

"Aunt Mayme, it's me, Alex. Art is my grandpa, and he is old, and really big." Mayme came even closer and held Alex's face in the palm of her hand.

"Mayme, Art is our sister Margaret's son. Yes, Art is our nephew too. But this is Alex, Art's grandson. This is Mary's child. He is our youngest nephew, and you love him very much, and he loves you." Carrie hesitated; she took a deep breath.

"Carrie, you know I can never understand that who is related to who, thing."

Alex thought, *I get it. I can't figure that stuff out either.*

"Mayme, you need to slow down. You know how you get when things happen quickly, and you get excited."

"Carrie, Art, I mean Alex; both of you, give me a moment. I forgot something in the bedroom. I will be right back." Alex looked at Carrie. He saw a tear run down her cheek; her hand quivered.

Mayme returned to the bedroom. The fan was still oscillating, but the room was considerably hotter, the humidity unbearable. She sat on her bed; her mind swirled in perplexity. She attempted to grasp what, only a few minutes ago, seemed clear to her. She reached for the bottle of Sambuca on the nightstand; she filled the shot glass, then slung it back like a cowboy in a saloon. She contemplated deeply on Alex. As her mind settled, her memories reorganized. Her fondness for Alex returned and filled her heart. She came out. "Okay Alex, Carrie, let's go to the park. I'm going to win our water fight today. Get your goggles, Art, I mean Alex. You are going to need them."

"I have a brand-new pair, Aunt Mayme. Mom said my head was getting too fat for my old ones. Let's go." Mayme knelt to give Alex a loving hug and a scratchy kiss on the cheek.

"I love you, Alex."

The Great Great Aunts from Prussia

"I love you too, Aunt Mayme." Alex hugged her around the neck with a big smile. Alex and Carrie struggled to bring Mayme to her feet, and off they went; Mayme in her 'Roaring Twenties' swimwear; Alex in his seashell speedo. Mayme and Alex strolled hand-in-hand; Carrie followed with two bath towels.

(As usual, the pool was crowded with grade-schoolers. It was the size of two big living rooms. The pool had no filtration system. Every hour, the whistle blew. The children were required to get out and sit on the side. The pool was dosed with a large quantity of chlorine, then mixed by everyone kicking their feet.)

Alex wasted no time jumping in. Mayme climbed down the steps slowly and feebly with her captivating smile on her face. The kids and mothers watched the 'Crazy old lady,' as she was known in the neighborhood. However, she and Carrie earned everyone's respect. They were a template for good neighbors. They were always there to help. Newcomers were skeptical, but quickly understood.

Mayme completed her descent and established her feet firmly on the pool's bottom. Alex approached her slowly. "Put your goggles on, Art, I mean Alex." As soon as he did, he was hit in the face by a splash from his animated aunt. Alex splashed back. Mayme shoved a splash at another little boy and, after seeing Alex splash her, he splashed her too.

The boy's mother darted poolside. She was new to the surrounding streets. "No, no, no, Ben. We do not splash adults, young man; apologize to the nice lady."

Mayme looked at the mother, smiled, and flung water at her, soaking her blouse. "C'mon, Mommy, join us and have some fun. He can splash me all he wants. I started it." Mayme turned towards the boys with her cute laugh. Soon, the whole pool was in a water fight.

Carrie sat on the park bench watching her sister create chaos wherever she went; some good, some questionable; but the questionable ones were increasing. Carrie's job was gaining in intensity. She knew she must protect Mayme from harming herself. It was times like these Carrie did not know whether to feel embarrassment or feel joy watching her sister play with Alex. It brought back fond memories of when they were little girls in Cologne, at least until...; She changed her thought.

Carrie could see Mayme was getting tired. She had been in the hot sun for over an hour. Her shoulders were beginning to drupe; she was leaning against the side. It was time to go home. She rose from the park bench and walked to the poolside. "Time to go, kids."

"No, Carrie. Can't we stay a little longer? Alex and I are having so much fun." Mayme was responding like any child, not wanting to stop playing; but Alex was getting bored with the pool. He took Mayme's hand and helped her up the steps. Carrie placed towels over their shoulders.

"Can I play on the slide and the swings for a while, Aunt Carrie, please?" Carrie could never resist his face, and he asked in such a cute whiney way.

Mayme intervened. "Art, I mean Alex, your Aunt Mayme needs to go home, but if Aunt Carrie wants to stay here with you, I can walk home by myself." Mayme needed her shot of Sambuca, then a nap. Those shots, naps, and memory lapses were increasing every day.

Carrie saw the fatigue on Mayme's face. "Sure Mayme, we will meet you at home. We won't be long. Mary should be there very soon. Tell her where we are."

"Okay." But as Mayme began to slowly walk away, she stopped and turned. "Carrie?"

"Yes, Mayme."

"Who is Mary?"

7

Departure from Heaven to Hell
"People, Class is in Session"

Cologne, Prussia
June 25, 1866
Monday

"Did you have a fun night? I hear your grandpa took you to the bowling alley."

"He did. It's kinda boring sometimes, but he buys me a lot of sodas and potato chips, and he gives me a lot of dimes to play pinball. But I want to hear about Langa…"

"Langensalza, I know, it is a big word; it is The Battle of Langenzalza."

"Yea, let's go, Aunt Carrier."

Morning arrived before the sun and breakfast was repeated with bread, blackberry jam, and coffee. While Ida helped Anna, the children playfully poked and prodded each other around the kitchen table as they waited to depart for the train station. As the first signs of daylight finally peered through the kitchen window, three large horse-drawn wagons and a carriage arrived in front of the Rothert home. A dozen soldiers guarded the wagons. Captain Heil, accompanied by two of his soldiers, knocked on the door. Ida graciously greeted them and showed them into the vestibule. Hearing their arrival, Joseph left his office, made his way through the back hallway, and into the kitchen. He looked at Maria, "Come Maria." She rose from the bench and followed her father without hesitation.

Joseph said his good mornings to all in the vestibule, and after doing so, he addressed his wife as if she were a private in the army. "Ida, pack breakfast for Maria and me? Our equipment and supplies must be loaded onto the wagons. Maria and I must verify all are present. We do not have time to eat. Thank you." Joseph went to his office; Captain Heil and Maria followed close behind.

The soldiers helped Joseph and Maria carry their gear outside. Most of the supplies were in the wagons from Maria's gatherings the day before. As far as personal items are concerned, Joseph and Maria had few. "Doctor, will you and your daughter take a quick look inside the wagons and confirm we have all you require?"

"From here on, Captain, refer to my head nurse as Nurse Rothert. She will need the respectful title when things get rough." Joseph was unemotional; Ida heard it from the hallway. She wanted to make one final attempt to stop her daughter from leaving Cologne. She felt Maria had already done enough for Prussia.

Maria and Joseph confirmed all supplies were present. Captain Heil gave them each a package. They went up the stairs with the packages under their arms. Ida was puzzled. The captain instructed Ida to gather her children. He led them to the carriage which would carry them to the train station where they would bid their farewells. The morning was cool for June. A slight mist caused Ida to cover herself and her children with woolen blankets. The smell was that of a wet animal. All were quiet, even the youngest of the children. They found the soldiers intimidating.

"Where are Father and Maria?" asked the youngest. "They are going with us, right?"

Ida had a curious frown on her face. "I am not sure what they are doing, child, but yes, they will be riding with us. We will leave when…" Ida stopped in mid-sentence as the front door opened. Joseph descended the marble stairway to the street. He was in full officer uniform with captain stripes, a hat, and a Red Cross banner around his arm. The children clapped and cheered.

"Oh Joseph," Ida whimpered. "You look so strong and handsome, but please do not allow them to take any more of my children. I could not bear it." She buried her face in her hands. Her oldest son embraced her.

Then Maria came out the door. Standing at the top of the stairs, she was grand. She was dressed in all white; shoes, stockings, dress, and a nurse's cap. Sewn onto the front of her uniform was a Red Cross. Her siblings, as well as Joseph, were stunned, and so proud. The children clapped and cheered once more. Ida was overwhelmed with emotion. Her daughter was now a woman. She looked powerful and mature, yet still, the thought of losing her in battle engulfed her soul.

Captain Heil approached. "Captain Rothert, Nurse Rothert, ride in the supply wagon with the other soldiers."

Ida stanchly rose to her feet. "No Captain, please, there is a spot next to me. Please give me a few more moments before you take my daughter from me; I beg of you."

Maria looked at her mother. She felt her pain. "Mother, I love you, and all my siblings; no one could love their family more. But the captain is not taking me from you; this is my choice. This is God's will. If I am ordered to ride with the soldiers, then that is what I must do." Joseph and Captain Heil looked at each other; they had subtle smiles upon their faces.

"Mrs. Rothert, I believe we can squeeze two more in your carriage. It would be most appropriate for you and your children to escort the good doctor and his head nurse to the train station. Please, hold your daughter in your arms and let her siblings be proud of her. We need more loyal and dedicated Prussians like these two." The captain saluted the family.

"Thank you, sir." Maria bowed her head in gratitude. The youngest of the boys popped up and saluted the captain in return.

Joseph squeezed the captain's arm and mouthed the words, "Bless you."

As the convoy began its trek to the train station, Ida and Maria cuddled under the blanket. Ida gazed at the wagons of soldiers. She could not imagine her little girl amid men fighting and killing each other. *No, this cannot be real. Tell me Lord, this is a bad dream*, she thought.

Arriving at the station, the mammoth engine gave out with a relieving belch of steam. The mist changed to a drizzle. The captain's men unloaded medical supplies into two passenger cars where they, and the Red Cross, would travel together. Joseph followed to supervise.

"Mrs. Rothert, you may move your family into that covered wagon to keep dry. He looked at Maria. "Your father needs your help, Nurse Rothert. Mrs. Rothert, she will return to say good-bye."

Ida moved her family into the wagon, but she remained outside. She watched men march past with guns on their shoulders. They were being jammed into box cars, but when she looked closer, all the men's faces changed. They weren't men; they were boys. Above the chaos, Ida heard a familiar voice and saw a hand waving. "Mrs. Rothert, oh, Mrs. Rothert, over here." The waving came from Otto Braun, little Otto Braun. He stood alongside his father, Pastor Braun, and his mother. She walked closer to see Otto's mother crying; they embraced. "I am sorry, Mrs. Braun. Maria told us about Otto's draft letter last Friday at dinner. Oh dear, he is too young, way too young, Mrs. Braun."

"Oh Ida, they just took him. They snatched him right out of my arms. They delivered the letter in person early Monday morning, then came to our house on Thursday. They put him into a wagon filled with other boys, and off they went. We were told we could say our goodbyes this morning on this platform. But Ida, what are you doing here? Your sons are too young to be drafted. Don't tell me the army broke the law and took one of them as well. Something is happening, and it is serious. I am so frightened."

"No, they did not take any of my sons, but they conscripted Joseph to be the head of the medical team and…" Ida choked.

"What is it, dear? It must be hard watching your husband leave for war again. But he came back unscathed from America. Those doctors are well behind the front lines." Mrs. Braun was trying to be delicate. She knew Joseph was scathed.

"No, Mrs. Braun, that's not it." Ida hesitated once more as she watched Mrs. Braun dry her eyes. "When our daughter, Maria, found out Otto was drafted, she came home Friday and informed us she joined the Red Cross, the organization where nurses help wounded soldiers on the battlefield."

Pastor Braun overheard the women's conversation, but Otto did not. It was time. The boys were pulled from their parents and loaded onto the train. But Otto was excited. He felt like a man for the first time in his life. It was an adventure. He quickly blended into the vast ocean of boys. Stretching her neck, Mrs. Braun made a futile effort to catch one last glimpse of her departing child. Without turning her head, she spoke, "Ida, I cannot imagine how you must feel. Your husband is a doctor and trained in warfare, but your daughter, that poor child." Mrs. Braun turned and held Ida firmly by the shoulders. "I have known your little Maria since she was baptized as an infant, and although I am frightened for her, I am overwhelmed by her courage and dedication to help boys like our Otto. You and your family have the Lord's deepest blessing."

Ida then saw Otto's innocent smile peek around the corner of the box car opening. "Goodbye, Mrs. Rothert. Give Maria my love. Tell her I will be home soon." Otto was unaware Joseph and Maria were two cars in front of him. He was about to discover war was the invention of Satan himself, and he was about to get a visit.

The train was ready to depart. The engine bell clanged; 'All aboard' echoed through the haze. Joseph and Maria finished their inventory and the whole family embraced. Emotions were mixed except for the love and respect felt for each other. Joseph made the good-byes quick and simple. They boarded. Neither Joseph nor Maria waived from the window as the train lumbered out of the station. For them, it was time to go to work.

Stopping to pick up more soldiers and supplies, the train to Langensalza would arrive the following morning. During that time, Joseph and Maria spent every moment teaching their three doctors and thirty Red Cross nurses the art of warfare medicine. Joseph did not ease up on Maria at any time. Her training was his focus in her teenage years. Now she needed to pass his knowledge on to the nurses while he trained the doctors. But he could not help but glance at her from time to time. In those brief moments, he realized the depth of love and respect he had for his "little girl." Joseph knew, once the fighting started, there was no time for feelings, only time for saving lives.

"So, Aunt Carrie, are you now gonna tell me about the war and stuff?" How do your mom and dad meet? And who wins the war? Is it the good guys?"

"Alex, it is supposed to rain all day today, and Mayme is not feeling well this morning. Do you want to play dominoes, or do you want me to tell you more about the war?"

"More."

8

The Fields Swarm with Confusion
The Red Cross is Prepared

Langensalza, Prussia
June 26, 1866
Tuesday

"Well, my love, today we visit Langensalza."

"Where the war started and your Mom and Dad meet?"

"Here we go."

It was twenty-four hours since Joseph and Maria departed from their comfortable family life in the City of Cologne. The massive iron horse stopped at countryside train stations along the Prussian landscape to jam more young draftees into the claustrophobic box cars. The train arrived midmorning in the quaint farming village of Langensalza. As the sun rose, the air became dense. The heat caused dehydration for the young soldiers crammed tightly together. Nausea and fatigue were obvious on their faces. Joseph, now addressed as Dr. Rothert, was near exhaustion as well. He and Maria spent the trip, both day and night, training inexperienced volunteers in the art of stitching, bandaging, and removing minor shrapnel and bullets. Their passenger car carried a pungent odor as the trainees practiced on skinned pigs and slaughtered rabbits, donated by the farmers of Cologne.

In Langensalza, the army pitched three tents for the Red Cross, then furnished them with cots and lanterns. Then they pitched one more containing six operating tables and a canvas tarp outside to shield wounded soldiers from the heat of the sun and moisture from the rain.

Like a colony of cutter ants, soldiers unloaded the medical supplies and stacked them in the corner of each tent. Maria organized the supplies needed for post-op; Joseph arranged the operatory to prepare for surgery.

While the systematic arrangement of the field hospital continued, a stark contrast surrounded the station; chaos was everywhere. Soldiers jumped from the box cars like rats fleeing a sinking ship. Most went directly to the fields to relieve themself. Unable to understand the barking of orders above the heaving of the steam engine, the young men cared only that they were out of their human fish tanks. Otto Braun was lost in this sea of confusion, so he drifted into a small group of men marching in loose formation toward a cluster of canvas tents. As they arrived, the soldiers were instructed to stand at attention in single file. The squad leader read his list of names. When he finished, Otto raised his hand.

"Sir, you didn't call my name. It is Otto, Otto Braun. You must have missed it?" Otto could feel anxiety welling in his throat.

"Sorry son, no Otto Braun on this list." The squad leader stared coldly at Otto.

"What should I do, sir?" The patrol leader laughed at Otto's childlike whine for help.

"To what patrol were you assigned, soldier?"

"The Ranger patrol, sir, I think. Or maybe it was the Rhinehart patrol. I forget." Otto was on the brink of panic.

"Go back to the train station, kid, and I don't know, ask somebody if you can spend the night with the little girls in town." This time the whole patrol laughed. Otto wanted to cry. He was embarrassed and confused. He was never away from home. He felt like a lost puppy dodging horses in the street.

"Yes sir, thank you, sir, I'll find my way." Otto saluted the officer and walked off, but he wanted to run all the way back to his bedroom in Cologne and hide under his bed. He strolled through the camp, hoping someone might help him. Finally, he came across an older soldier sitting alone on the hillside, his back propped against a tall oak tree. He approached the soldier.

Joseph was given top secret information from Von Bismarck when he was assigned the task of training the Red Cross. Langensalza was to be a rehearsal for the real battles to come. This was only a decoy to block the Hanoverians while a major part of Prussian Army gathered elsewhere. Joseph was part of hoax, especially to the Hanoverian spies.

Joseph and Maria approached the captain in charge. "Captain," asked Joseph. "Have you been briefed on when the fighting will begin? How much time do I have to prepare my staff?" Joseph wanted an update to confirm Von Bismarck's strategy had not changed.

"Dr. Rothert, that is between General Flies and Head command."

"Father?" Maria interrupted.

"Nurse Rothert, please address me as Dr. Rothert until we return home and enjoy our precious Anna's hasenpfeffer." He smiled. She reciprocated. And that would be the last time Maria and Joseph allowed themselves to smile in public. "How may I help you?"

"You asked the captain to give you an idea of when the fighting will begin?"

"Yes, I did; continue please."

"Then I must address an issue. There are nurses who must remain in camp and perform stitching, bandaging, and the cleansing of wounds, correct?"

"Yes, that is correct."

"And others will be needed in surgery and post-op."

"That is also true. What is your question?"

"Your manual has a section on triage nurses, but you have not trained any of us for that duty." Joseph, knowing there would not be a battle in Langenzalza, deprioritized triage training. "I wish to be trained to evaluate the wounded on the battlefield." Joseph felt his first twinge of paternal emotion. Until now, it was the medics duty to merely gather the wounded. Now, it was the duty of the Red Cross nurses to evaluate the wounded on the battlefield. His daughter would put herself in a position where she could be killed by the enemy.

Joseph knew what was in his manual; and he knew Maria knew. However, when he wrote it, he never imagined his daughter to be one who would volunteer and place herself in mortal danger. The approval of her request would change his daughter's life forever or, God forbid, end it. Without hesitation, he answered, "Yes, Nurse Rothert, if that is your desire, I will train ten of you to evaluate severities, but those nurses must volunteer. As you are my daughter, I must warn you. A triage nurse on a battlefield must not, I repeat, must not treat, or remove the most severely wounded first. They must be your lowest of priority." Joseph stopped and stared into the innocent face of his daughter, knowing it may be the last time. With what he was about to say, she would be a woman with tainted dreams and troubled memories for the rest of her life. "It will become your decision, and yours alone, to which soldiers you remove to treat, and which you leave to die."

Maria was stunned. "Why would I leave a soldier to die?"

"Look at the village; it is small. The farmers and merchants can supply you with only a limited number of wagons to transport the wounded back to me. And you will have a limited number of medics to carry them to those transports."

"Are you saying …?"

"Yes, it will be left to the triage nurses to make decisions of life and death, and you will make them many times. I will train your staff to recognize the symptoms of a man with no chance of survival, with or without surgery. You must learn to recognize the gurgling sound of their lungs filling with blood, the grayish hue of their skin as they lose oxygen. You must look for stomach wounds where organs are exposed and unrepairable. And you must recognize the smell of a perforated bowel and other organ fluids. Send me only those I can save; you must leave those we cannot. They and the dead will be gathered last."

Joseph was almost unrecognizable. He was always loving and caring, a saint in her eyes. But this was Dr. Joseph Rothert, a man who witnessed a bloody, horrific civil war in America. She remembered the days since his return; he had changed, but he hid it well. Maria fought back her tears.

"Don't you dare drop a tear. Your job is to save as many lives as possible, but you cannot save all of them. That is our job in wartime. Crying comes later when you are in your room at home with no one around, like I do when you all go to the market."

Maria held her head high; she stared into her father's eyes. "Yes sir, I understand. You are saying, when all this is over, I will be proud of the entire team for the lives we saved, but I will always be sad for those I left behind."

"Not sad, haunted my child. You will be haunted by faces who visit you in your nightmares. Meet me in the operatory in one hour with our triage volunteers, but only ones you feel are emotionally capable of handling the task. You must explain to them what I told you before you bring them. We do not have time to deal with the weak in their position. It would be unfair to the soldiers."

"See you in an hour, Doctor." Maria left the tent with a different attitude from when she entered. She was scared, not for herself, but for those poor boys she must leave behind to die alone on the battlefield, so far away from their loved ones.

"Wow, your grandfather was mean. He let people die?"

"No child, that is why war is so terrible. He saved a lot of lives, as did my mother."

"But I heard you say there was not going to be a battle. Is there or isn't there?"

"Well, we will find out, won't we." She kissed Alex on the forehead, then went to check on Mayme.

9

August Does Not Like What He Sees

Prussian Army Encampment
Bad Langensalza
June 26, 1866
Tuesday

"When does your father come back into the story and meet your mother?"

"Are you ready for that, Alex?"

"C'mon Aunt Carrie. But there's not going to be a lot of kissy stuff, right?"

"Later in the story, but not yet. I will warn you. Okay, here we go, my sweet. But remember, it gets kind of rough from here on."

"I'm ready, but no kissing."

Looking from the hillside of the encampment, dense fog sprawled as still as death in the grassy valley below. Mildew-stained tents pocked the woods. They were spread out to make it appear the army was larger than it was. The air was filled with the begrimed smell of smoldering campfires, brewing coffee, and an occasional chunk of venison or rabbit on the end of sharpened tree branches. It was June 26, 1866, outside of Langensalza, in the Prussian province of Saxony. King Wilhelm ordered nine thousand Prussian troops to make haste to this remote area and, with their sheer presence, block the Hanoverian troops from marching westward to unite with their Bavarian allies. King Wilhelm needed only a short window of time to gather his troops and attack Hanover from the north. It would leave them with no path to escape.

In the conflict known as the Austro-Prussian War, Hanover's purpose in joining Bavaria was to defeat Prussia and bring the Austrian government into power over all the Germanic-speaking provinces. This united power would result in the country of Germany. But rather than attacking, the Hanoverians were given an exaggerated number of troops by their spies creeping through the camp. To the Prussian foot soldiers, their purpose on this hillside was unknown; anything they spoke of was pure conjecture.

August sat under a beautifully seasoned pin oak; he peered down at his army's camp below. He kept his rifle close in anticipation of a sniper attack through the fog. The seasoned soldiers who participated in previous wars took this time to quiet their minds and think of nothing at all.

As he sat alone waiting for his mundane breakfast of coffee and oatmeal, a soldier with the countenance and body of an adolescent stood over him; his soft, pale hands trembled as if in winter; his frightened blue eyes open wide. "What is your name, sir? Mine is Otto."

"My name is August, August Wehmeyer." Otto needed someone who exuded the same confidence as his big brothers in Cologne.

"You look a lot older than me, sir. I am the youngest of four brothers." Otto continued to stand; his obtuse request to sit was not granted. August neither needed nor did he want a boy disturbing his peace.

"Look kid, my name is August, not sir. Call me sir again, and I could be picked off by a sniper or have one of these spies creeping around cut my throat." August was intentionally rude. Otto felt ashamed. He could not say the right thing to anyone this morning.

"Spies? What makes you think there are spies in our camp?" asked Otto glancing quickly in every direction like a fawn who smelled a wolf.

"It is part of war. The Hanoverians need to know what we have over here before they attack."

"What we have, like what?"

August could not believe this kid was this naïve. "Like how many soldiers, how many cannons, how many horses. Come on, why else would they be snooping around?" August continued to scan uphill and down, then he stared back into the fog.

"Yes, but they're just looking around, sir? They don't kill anybody, do they? It's not like they're soldiers."

"Stop calling me sir, kid. I will start calling you sir, and I'm going to salute you a few times. Your throat will be slit somewhere in the night as you take a piss. They kill officers for good reason; with no officers, we have chaos. But most of our officers are idiots anyway. Spies are watching us right now. That's why I stay by myself, so nobody thinks I am of any importance. Get it?" August thought *enough of this kid; time for him to go.*

"Oh, I'm so sorry, sir, I mean August. I had no idea that could happen; seems like cheating to me."

"It is cheating. And if a spy is caught, he doesn't get detention and stay after class. They are hung by their neck and left dangling, a reminder to other spies what we do if we catch them. Look down there near the edge of camp, just above the fog." August pointed. Otto caught glimpse of a swaying body with two turkey vultures picking at its face.

Otto lost his breath. It was his first sight of death in his life. "I was just being respectful, really I was. You remind me of my big brothers at home, that's all. One's name is Marcus. He is the oldest. He kind of looks like you." He paused. "Maybe I should…" Otto again felt he was doing and saying everything wrong. Maybe it would be better to hang out with a kid his own age.

At the same time, August felt Otto's helplessness. He remembered the times he protected his little brother, Henry. August interrupted, "No, no, kid, wait. I'm sorry. Did they not teach you anything in boot camp?"

"Boot camp, what's that? Two Fridays ago, I graduated from High School. On Monday, they delivered a draft notice to my house. Thursday, they picked a bunch of us up in a wagon. They shaved our heads, gave us this uniform, and sort of showed us how to shoot it."

"What do you mean 'sort of' showed you how to shoot it?"

"Well, they gave us the rifle already loaded, pointed us at a target, and we pulled the trigger. They haven't given us any bullets of our own yet."

"August rolled his eyes. "Then what?"

"Yesterday, I left Cologne in a box car." August began to understand what was happening around him. "They jammed us in. It was so tight we had to squeeze through each other to get outside between the cars to shit or vomit. If we had to piss, we just did it on the floor. We were all scared, so there was a lot of diarrhea. Today, I'm here in these woods, wherever these woods are."

August spat on the ground; he picked up a rock and threw it at a tree twenty feet away. Otto felt August's frustration. "I'm sorry I got down on you, kid. None of this is your fault. But if we are going into battle, God help us."

The Great Great Aunts from Prussia

"Who would we be fighting?"

"The Hanoverians are on the other side of those valleys a few kilometers away. Rumor has it, they just finished their summer training exercises, and they are preparing to march. We have spies, too." But August thought *we now outnumber them, but do they know our troops are untrained? Perhaps we are here only to block their path. Oh God, please let that be it.*

"I'm still confused. Why don't they attack us now if they are trained and ready to move?"

"I am sure the Hanoverians are confused. They can't figure out why we doubled our troops in the last three days. But they don't know your training is a joke."

"What does that mean?"

"That means, if the fighting starts, it will not be a Prussian victory; it will be a massacre of Prussian children. Now, sit down and stop swinging that rifle all over the place. They go off accidently, and I don't want to be shot by some dumb-ass draftee. Put your rifle next to you on the ground like I have mine, pointing downhill and away from the tents. And never allow your gun or your ammunition to be out of your arm's reach."

"August, don't worry about my gun going off. Remember, they never gave me any bullets. I don't even know how to load it even if I had some. Can you teach me?"

August shook his head as he looked at the ground. *On my,* August thought, *our army is not only untrained, but totally impotent.* It was pitiful. Kids like Otto poured in every few hours; they swarmed the camp like a herd of lost goats, not knowing where they should be or what they should do. Otto needed someone to help him through his anxiety, and August's help might save his life. He would want somebody to help Henry if he was ever put in this perilous situation.

Otto sat and followed August's instructions. He taught him how to clean his gun, how to load it, and how to aim it. "The gun you have in your hand is our biggest advantage. It is called a Dreyse needle gun. It is known as a breechloader. Its advantage is we can reload without standing up. The Hanoverians still use muzzleloaders; they need to stand after every shot. Plus, we can fire three shots to everyone of theirs."

"So, we can sit when we shoot, right?"

"Not only can we sit, but we can lie on the ground when we reload. That makes us small targets. This gun gives us a lot of confidence in a battle, but I hope not too much." August was hoping Otto was feeling better with the training, but the guns were one thing; inexperienced boys shooting them was another.

"Sounds like you've been in the army a long time. Do you really think we are in real danger, August?" Otto swiveled his head in each direction.

"In danger, kid? Although you boys are untrained, assuming they give you all ammunition, you are soldiers with a guns. And over there is an army of young soldiers with guns as well, and the point of this war thing is to kill each other. That's how it works; everyone's in danger."

"How many troops do we have? How many do they have? Are we attacking them or are they attacking us?"

"Otto, officers don't want foot soldiers talking purpose or strategy; we never know for certain what is going to happen." August placed his finger on his lip to shush Otto as two soldiers passed by. But August knew for certain this boy was not a fighter. He appeared to come from a "soft" life. August guessed his mother and father were teachers of some sort. He was close. They were clergy. August's father, on the other hand, fought in the Napoleonic Wars, then learned the skill of throwing pottery. He made commercial vases, bowls, plates, and jewelry. It was hard work in the heat of the kilns. They lived in a rough working-class neighborhood. Otto was now in a world he only read about in history books. He was scared and confused; and it was about to get bad; very bad.

10

Plans Change and the World Changes
The Eve of
The Battle of Langensalza

Langensalza, Prussia
June 26, 1866
Tuesday

"General Flies, I have a telegram from Field Marshal Moltke, sir." The corporal handed the telegram to his general, saluted, then left the tent as quickly as he arrived. Flies opened the telegram from the head of the Prussian army. It read:

> *General Flies, we are moving troops to the north of Hanover. Hold your position. Do not attack unless further ordered. Destroy this telegram immediately.*

"What is it, sir," asked the lieutenant, "new orders?"

Flies walked slowly with belligerence to the candle on his desk. He touched the flame to the corner of the telegram. He watched the paper burn, holding it just long enough to feel a welcome pain in his fingertips. With arrogance in his eyes, he dropped the ashes to the ground and smeared them into the dirt beneath his heel. He walked to his open tent flap; he stared at the sun setting behind the hilltops. He envisioned another medal on his chest.

Flies thought t*he old man has been in command too long. We can defeat them with our rifles alone, not to mention our artillery and horses. I refuse to pass up this opportunity for glory. My name will be in history books. I will take over command.*

"Send for my officers, Lieutenant." They were in his tent within minutes. "New orders gentlemen, time to move. Ready the men to march at three hundred hours." Flies would be the only one aware of his acts of insubordination against the Chief Field Marshal himself.

It was the infancy of Wednesday June 27 at three A.M. The squad leader poked his head into August's tent and whispered, "Get your things, men. Leave the tent where it stands. We're moving out. Be silent and unload your rifles." August knew what was happening. Otto had moved into August's tent with this group of experienced soldiers, but only because no one told him where he was supposed to sleep. All knew what was happening. It was time to attack.

"August, we are moving out to where?"

"Keep your voice down; talk to me only in a whisper. This is it, kid. Get your gun and the ammo I gave you?"

"Yes sir, I mean August. I guess now is really not the time to call you sir." Otto tried to fake a smile, but his fear was obvious. August ignored his comment. "Why do we need to unload our rifles? You told me to always keep it loaded and by my side."

"Sounds like a surprise attack. If anyone's gun goes off accidently, we just set off an alarm clock for the Hanoverians."

Four abreast, the Prussian infantry marched quietly down the hillside and into the fog. Otto stayed close to August, mimicking his every move. They remained in total silence. Even though he had no breakfast, Otto vomited on the back of the boots of the soldier in front of him. The soldier glanced at Otto over his shoulder but kept marching. Otto peered at August from the corner of his eye expecting a frown, but he was smiling. The soiled soldier was as young as Otto.

The infantry was quiet, only an occasional branch cracked beneath its feet. And from the rear, only the occasional whinny of a horse was faintly heard. The troops exited the fog of the first valley, then marched up and over two more crests. It was four kilometers in total.

Climbing the third grassland, the infantry halted. The officers ordered half the soldiers to line the crest on their stomachs. The second half were instructed to kneel behind them. The sun rose in the east casting a pinkish-purple glow crept onto the horizon. As light dominated the darkness, Otto saw the troops span a quarter mile, far enough back from the hilltop to be hidden from the enemy's view. In the silence, Otto heard songbirds singing and a soft breeze caressed his cheeks. Small patches of smoke could be seen over the next hilltop. The Prussians were positioned perfectly, for when the Hanoverians charged the hill, the Prussians could shoot downward at their musket-loading enemy.

"Soldiers, load your weapons. Cannons, move into position." When General Flies saw all was set, he gave the order. "Cannons---FIRE." Their shells cruised over top of the next hill and into the enemy camp. In the distance, drums and bugles sounded the alarm. The explosions caused their horses to rear and whinny. The shouting of orders could be heard. Chaos was assumed.

"What now, August? Did we win? What's next? Is it over?" Otto thought he could talk now; there was no more surprise.

"That's just the first round." The cannons reloaded and fired again, then a third time. Otto envisioned the Hanoverians scrambling and running away. He smiled with a naïve sense of victory. But suddenly, cannon shells exploded behind him, even behind the Prussian cavalry. Tree limbs snapped, crashing to the ground. Dirt and pebbles covered Otto's back as put his arms over his head. He waited for August's instruction.

"What's going on? They're firing over our heads, but they are missing us. Are they just bad shots?" August knew precisely what they were doing. The Hanoverians were ready for them. Their spies did their job. They had been ready for the attack for days. They found the influx of Prussian troops suspicious, but it was Flies' ego that made the attack predictable.

"They're shooting howitzers. This isn't good." It was the first time Otto saw fear in August's face.

"What's a howitzer, and why is that bad?"

"It is a type of cannon which shoots with a high trajectory. It is mainly used to get behind walls of castles and fortresses, or in our case, terrain. We've been shooting our cannons from the top of the hillside. Our cannons are not howitzers; they shoot at a low trajectory. But since they are up here, we can shoot straight across and into their camp. That would work if they were charging, but that's not what they're doing." August, unaware Flies disobeyed orders, figured the Field Marshal miscalculated and marched his troops into a death trap. He must have counted on the Hanoverians charging in masse over the crest. Their guns and cannons would desecrate the Hanoverian troops. But it was Flies who was wrong, not the Field Marshal.

"I'm still confused. Why are they shooting behind us? Why not at us?"

"Listen closer. The explosions keep getting closer. Eventually they will force us to charge down the hill into the open valley. That is where this battle will be fought."

"So, what do we do now?"

"We sit and wait for the command."

"What command?" August was scared, but more for the life of this young boy. August thought, *I do not want to die, but I do not want him to die. He is so much like Henry.*

"Stay close and do exactly what I do."

As the cannon shells came closer and closer behind them, the order to move to the hillside was given. When they did, the Hanoverians appeared at the top across from them. They fired upon the advancing soldiers.

"What do we do now, August?" Otto asked again.

"Sit next to me, fire at them, then reload. Do it over and over. We can load and fire three times faster than they can. Let's pick those bastards off one at a time. Aim the way I taught you, and fire at will."

The Prussians picked off row after row of Hanoverians as they shot their muskets. But the howitzer shells continued to explode closer behind them. They were being forced to the floor of the valley. This was where the Hanoverians wanted them. Suddenly, from the right, the thunder of hooves was heard; it vibrated the ground. Soldiers on horseback attacked with swords and pistols. The Prussian ran down the valley to escape. As they turned the bend, a company of soldiers created a musket barrier. One round of musket balls wiped out those who ran the fastest to escape. The Prussians opened fire as the muskets reloaded. With horses behind and muskets in front, the remaining route was to scramble back up the hill through the howitzer barrage.

Flies saw he was overrun. He was so upset he fainted from his horse. No one was in charge. His lieutenant sounded retreat. Some soldiers made it through the valley and escaped back to Langenzalza; others did not.

August and Otto climbed the hill with howitzers continuing to fire at the crest. A shell hit the top of a huge cedar and exploded; jagged splinters filled the air, branches crashed to the ground. August turned to peer at the chaos below. Soldiers were surrendering. They dropped their rifles and knelt with their hands behind their heads.

The smell of gunpowder burned in August's nostrils; smoke filled his lungs. His ears rang. He called out to Otto, "Drop your weapon kid, and put your hands behind your head." But when August looked, Otto was sprawled on his back in the pine straw. A cedar branch clipped by a howitzer shell pierced his thigh, pinning him to the ground."

Thinking only of Otto, and with his rifle still in his hand showing no sign of surrender, he sprinted to aid his little friend. "No, kid, no. You'll be all right?" But as August rushed to the boy, one last shell exploded in the treetops; splinters pierced his eyes. As he reached for his face, a Hanoverian on horseback shot a bullet through his shoulder; it exited the other side, shattering his collarbone. He then cracked August on the crown of his head with the butt of his pistol, knocking him unconscious. August's skull bleed, blood pooled in the soil beneath his cheek.

The battle was over. The surrender flag was raised. The Hanoverians won a quick and decisive victory. Flies took 9,000 untrained boys and pitted them against 19,000 well-trained and well-armed Hanoverians. In the end, due to their rifles and quick surrender, the Prussians lost only 170 men, including eleven officers. The Hanoverians lost 378 men but captured 907. However, the battle prevented the Hanoverians from joining the Bavarians in time. Prussia won the war in seven weeks which led to the unification of the Germanic-speaking provinces under the rule of King Wilhelm I. Germany would evolve into a great world power.

"Wow, Aunt Carrie, how do you remember all that stuff?"

"My mother and father told us this story many times of how they met. Then, when I was older, I studied it in history books."

"So, did your father die?"

"Alex honey, I wouldn't be here if he would have died, now would I?"

"Oh yea, what was I thinking. So, he was blinded by those splinters. Did he ever see again?"

"I will give you a hint. He became a very famous blind man."

"What did he do that made him famous?"

Carrie smiled. "Time to stop. Tell you more tomorrow."

11

It is Time to Wait But for How Long And for What?

Langensalza, Prussia
June 26, 1866
Tuesday

"Is it time for them to meet, Aunt Carrie?"
"Getting close."

Joseph and his colleagues finished their final inspection of the hospital to ensure all supplies and instruments were in place. Now came the grueling period of waiting for their skills and training to override the agony of pain and avoid death. Meanwhile, soldiers sat anxiously in the grass and patches of bare earth. Throughout the encampment, muffled whimpers emanated from homesick boys attempting to remain unheard.

"Dr. Rothert, are you and your people prepared to take care of our soldiers in the case a battle ensues?" asked the captain as he returned from inspecting his untrained troops.

"How do your troops look, Captain?" Joseph knew the new recruits were young, but perhaps not all were plucked from the arms of their mothers.

"They resemble schoolboys on recess. Some think they are only playing soldier with toy guns, while others hide in their tents sobbing. Doctor, if a battle comes to fruition, perhaps we will need pediatricians instead." The captain removed his hat and ran his hand through his wet, greasy hair.

"A body is a body, Captain. We are ready to do everything we can to help your soldiers." Joseph appeared confident to the captain, only because he knew a battle was unlikely.

"Dr. Rothert, if your preparations are complete, assemble your team and meet me on the road behind your operatory. Dinner will be served shortly." Joseph frowned in perplexity. He had not thought of dinner, but with the suggestion, he was famished.

When the team assembled, the captain led them down a winding dirt road until they arrived at a quaint Lutheran church. They were greeted with handshakes, hugs, and curtseys by the peaceful people of Langensalza. They were led inside; they were informed a meal was prepared in their honor consisting of vegetables, sauerbraten with gingersnap gravy, and, like every Prussian meal, sauerkraut.

The pastor's wife interjected, "Allow me to show you to the rectory where fine people may clean up from your long train ride and exhausting day of preparation. Allow us to wash those beautiful white uniforms. We expect a breezy evening. They will dry by morning."

Joseph addressed the pastor's wife. "Ma'am, I am sure clean uniforms would be a pleasure for my nurses, but from this moment on, we must be ready to perform our duties at any time. I must insist they prefer dirty over wet."

"Perhaps my people can take a broom to them, then wipe them with a damp cloth." To the pastor's wife, it seemed a reasonable compromise for cleanliness.

"Ma'am, I must be blunt. We appreciate your gracious offer, but at some point, the stains on our uniforms will not be dirt and dust, the stains will be blood. That is when you may help, however, the scrubbing of blood may be quite difficult for those who are faint of heart. Each of my nurses has two uniforms. We will accept your laundering offer when necessary." Joseph continued to act as if a battle was imminent.

"I thank you for your honesty, Doctor. I believe there will be some members of our parish unable to help with the cleaning, but they certainly can cook." They exchanged respectful smiles.

It was a solemn dinner, not one of frivolity. The team was exhausted. The pastor blessed the food, and all prayed for the safety of the men on both sides. The townspeople knew from other battles in their long history, their town may be invaded and overrun.

Joseph rose to his feet. "Ladies and gentlemen, we graciously thank you for your hospitality. And while our days stay peaceful, we offer our medical services to your town free of charge." The citizens clapped in appreciation. "But it has been a stressful day for us, so we must return to our camp and enjoy a restful night of sleep. Thank you and bless you all."

The group followed Joseph and the captain down the road in buckboards filled with clean blankets and pillows. It was nine o'clock. The team fell asleep without delay. Maria prayed for courage and wisdom, but her eyes shut before her amen arrived.

The Earth Trembled
The Skies Rumbled
Judgment Day Began for Many a Young Man

The Battle of Langensalza
Part 1
June 27, 1866
Wednesday

"Are you ready, Alex? This is my favorite part. My mother and father each told this story a little differently since this is where they met for the first time."

"I'm ready, Aunt Carrie. Let's go!"

"Dr. Rothert, sir, Dr. Rothert, wake up." Joseph opened his eyes to a softly lit kerosene lantern. He was unable to grasp where he was or who this strange man might be waking him from his deep, dreamless sleep.

"Who are you son, and where am I?"

"I am Corporal Schmidt. General Flies lieutenant sent me," whispered the corporal.

"What is it, Corporal? Is it morning? It appears to be dark outside." Joseph sat up on the edge of his cot, stretched his arms, and yawned. "Is someone sick?"

"No sir, it's time." The young corporal's voice quivered as his hand touched Joseph's forearm. His touch was as cold as that of a dead man.

"Come son, what do you mean it's time? Spit it out." Joseph was irritated with the vagueness.

"The troops are moving out, sir; it is three hundred hours. They are marching on the Hanoverian camp. They will attack at daybreak. Their camp is four kilometers from here." The boy raised the wick of his lantern to extend more light.

"Are you telling me to prepare for wounded soldiers by midmorning?" No one knew of his relationship with Von Bismarck since the American Civil war, and no one knew he wrote the textbooks on warfare medicine. In the last two weeks, he and Von Bismarck communicated frequently. Joseph was confused. "Tell the lieutenant we will be ready. We will have nurses, medics, and wagons follow his troops. Tell him they will remain a safe distance from the front line until the gunfire and shelling ceases."

"Yes sir, Dr. Rothert." The young soldier saluted Joseph, then turned to exit.

"And Corporal, be sure Flies understands none of my nurses enter the battlefield until the fighting ends. I will not place them in any unnecessary danger." Joseph never had nurses in the field; no one had. He would not allow them to be wounded or captured. They all volunteered courageously, including his daughter.

"Yes sir." The corporal sped back to the command tent.

Joseph continued to position himself on the edge of his cot. He thought back to the previous weeks. *This cannot be. Von Bismarck told me we are merely a decoy to stop the Hanoverians from uniting with the Bavarians. He told me he drafted these boys only to inflate the troop size for the Hanoverian spies. General Flies would be ordered to hold his position, not attack. Von Bismarck would never let these boys be slaughtered. Oh Ida, forgive me. I would not have let Maria come if I knew she would be in real danger. The Red Cross was sent here to train for the future, as well as be part of the pretense."*

Joseph woke the doctors and explained the situation. He went to the nurses' tent and ordered Maria to ready for battle. Maria passed the word. When all were assembled, Joseph and the doctors entered the operatory. Joseph spoke. "Nurses, the army is moving out and will attack the Hanoverian camp at daybreak. That means, by midmorning, we will be immersed in the wounded and dying. Triage nurses, you will travel on wagons and buckboards to the battlefield, but you do not set foot on it until the officers tell you the fighting is over. Is that understood?"

No one spoke. All eyes were locked on Joseph. Maria's hands began to shake; she sat on them so her father could not see her fear.

"Once you are cleared, triage nurses, with the help of your medics, will comb the battlefield for wounded. You must only treat Prussian soldiers in accordance with the Red Cross treaty, not the enemy. And you will only bring us men who, in your personal evaluations, have a chance of survival. Send to the wagons on foot those who need stiches, splints, or the remove of minor shrapnel. When possible, send them back on foot. Save the wagons for the seriously wounded." The nurses were focused. They volunteered for a reason, and this was it. They knew their purpose. They were ready.

"Triage nurses, I will repeat. Do not send anyone back with a wound you believe to be fatal. Use your boot protocol. If they are still alive when we gather the dead, we will do what we can. You have been bestowed with the power of God. You must make decisions over who lives and who dies. You will never be the same after this day.

Just remember, by passing over a mortally wounded soldier, you saved someone from dying. God bless you all. I am proud to serve with every one of you. I have confidence in your abilities, and I have love in my heart for your beautiful souls."

As Joseph left the tent, he saw lanterns like lightning bugs in the town. Word was passed. They prepared their buckboards, wagons, and horses for their part of the mission. Within an hour, supplies were loaded along with stretchers for the strongest and most durable of soldiers, the medics. All soldiers could shoot a rifle, but not all could carry grown men on two wooden poles and a piece of canvas.

The waggoneers were instructed to be as silent as the bewitching hour surrounding them. This was a surprise attack. They were to move slowly so as not to stir up dust. All was in place, and General Flies was confident he would defeat his enemy and rise to historical fame. Joseph assumed this was Von Bismarck's new strategy, but it did not seem like him to endanger untrained boys. He thought, *if I knew there would be a battle, would I have refused Maria's enlistment? No, I would have allowed it. It is her life now.*

It would be a few hours before any wounded returned. Joseph made his way to the communication tent; he sent a telegram.

"Otto Von Bismarck. This is Joseph Rothert. I do not doubt your military strategies, however, I am confused by your decision to attack this morning. My Red Cross team is ready."

Within thirty minutes a telegram returned, "Joseph, that contradicts my direct orders to Flies. I will handle this in the proper manner. Please keep this between the two of us. For troop morale, I will handle it quickly. And my God bless our boys."

Snaking through the hills and valleys, two dozen makeshift ambulances driven by farmers, and pulled by plow horses, made their way to the unspeakable. Some nurses rode patiently in the backs of wagons while others marched alongside. Two-man medic teams marched with stretchers on their shoulders and prepared for the signal which would launch them into action. This was a time in history. The Red Cross was about to be baptized in the blood of Prussian soldiers.

Two soldiers on horses stopped the convoy, preventing them from being seen by the enemy. They would receive a signal when the fighting was over, but there was still an unanswered question. How protective would those Red Cross uniforms be on a real battlefield? The Austrians and their Hanoverian allies were yet to sign the Red Cross treaty.

From the wagons, they saw cannons and riflemen below the crest of the next hill. They saw soldiers on horseback filling the valley in front of them. Crystal-tinted sunlight with a peaceful elegance illuminated the tops of trees on the ridge in front of the convoy. Then, the echoing discharge of cannon fire broke the serenity, followed by another, and then another. As prepared as the nurses were, and as courageous as they had become in the past few days, gasps exuded down the line of wagons. Hugs of fear sprung spontaneously. Six town women jumped from the wagons and swiftly fled on foot for the village. The plow horses reared, displaying their own form of fright.

Maria perched on the seat of the front wagon. Her posture was one of strength, her face one of dignity. She resembled a concert pianist about to strike the first chord. She was excited, scared, and anxious at the same time. She was focused and ready to move forward; there was no turning back. She stood and held her arms skyward, signaling everyone to stay in place. She called out. "Be ready to move on my signal." She saw gunpowder rise like a forest fire from the next valley. Prussian forces were positioned at the top of the ridge. The signalers on horseback moved from the crest for protection. Enemy fire was returned via cannons, striking the hill in front of them. They were still out of range.

Within minutes, continuous reports were heard from the valley beyond. The air was saturated with the smell of gunpowder; the convoy covered their noses in their sleeves. Cannon fire continued, but was moving further away. The sound of gunshots lasted for thirty minutes, followed by the yelling of soldiers and the stampeding of horses.

Then, to Maria's left, she heard a simultaneous blast of musket fire, followed by Prussian soldiers pouring over the crest to the north, one-quarter kilometer down the valley. Soldiers retreated everywhere. Then, a few sporadic cannon explosions were followed by a dead eerie silence.

Maria watched the signalers. One waved a white flag, the other motioned to her it was time for the convoy to approach. The battle was over; the Prussians were quickly defeated. The Hanoverians were prepared for the attack and outnumbered the Prussians two to one. Maria and her team struck up the horses; the wagons headed to the battlefield. No one knew what they would encounter, but all knew they would need every bit of strength and courage to face what are known as the horrors of war.

Maria took her wagon alone to the crest. She descended from her bench and walked through cannon-splintered trees and branches. Reaching the other side, she gazed upon the grassy slope. It was horrific. It was beyond her imagination. Bodies were strewn down the valley. She heard men and boys crying, groaning, rolling on the ground in pools of their own blood. The sound of wounded horses belched their final whinnies as they struggled unsuccessfully to get to their feet.

In the distance, she saw the Prussian soldiers herded down the valley, two abreast; their hands folded on top of their heads. She heard the unnerving thuds of a musket butt smashed into Prussian soldiers' temples. The Hanoverians captured over nine hundred prisoners. Maria wanted to run and return to Anna's kitchen for milk and cookies. She wanted to vomit. But she was in command. With fortitude, she knew she must embrace the role entrusted to her by her father and to which she volunteered. She embraced it with all her heart. Within moments, she evaluated the situation; her courage soared. It was time to move into action. It was time to fire their angelic cannons

Maria hurried back to the convoy and yelled down the line. "It's not pretty folks. They need all of us. Let us see how many boys we can save." Those who waited all their lives for this moment clapped and cheered, but the jubilance was about to shrivel like a grape in the sunshine. "I need triage nurses and medics to come to the first three wagons. Medics, prepare your stretchers. Non-triage nurses, stay by the wagons for when the medics bring our wounded to you." How Maria knew to make such competent commands in a situation never performed by anyone in history was as strange to her as it was to those around her.

With red crosses on their arms and uniforms the first wave of nurses spread out like ants swarming an anthill. The Hanoverians stared at this strange sight. The nurses ignored them, concentrating on their duty at hand. The general watched from his horse. He was approached by his field officers.

"General, who are those women, and what are they doing here? Shall we gather them as POWs? They are clearly not helping our wounded, only the Prussians."

"No, we must leave them alone. By treaty, they are not permitted to treat our wounded. I was alerted they would be here. It is an international organization called the Red Cross. Our government has not yet signed the pact, so, in theory, we could capture them. But since they are under a flag of surrender, we cannot kill them."

"Good, we will gather them up then. We can force them to take care of our boys in a number of ways, if you know what I mean." The officers smirked perversely.

"Men, I agree. We certainly could use them, but no." The general was adamant. "I will report back to our field marshal about this. Maybe that will knock some sense into their stubborn political heads and sign the pact. We could use brave women like them. If we abuse them in any way, we will bring on the world's condemnation." The officers were disappointed with the answer. "If anyone hurts or even touches a Prussian woman, you will be in the stockade for a long, long, time. Is that understood?" The general stared at the blood-stained white dresses scurrying through the slaughterhouse. He wanted a medical team of his own on that field.

Medics brought the wounded to the loading area to be treated for their wounds. Those that could walk were sent back to camp on foot. Others were loaded onto the wagons and taken to the operatory. Some soldiers cried in pain, some screamed in pain, and some were despondent.

Maria observed the lines of captured soldiers. The POWs were extensive; most were uninjured. The severely wounded were ignored. The Hanoverians had their own to treat with limited caregivers. Maria and her nurses began to feel safe. The nurses scoured the field for those soldiers alive and treatable. Maria approached a soldier lying on his stomach in a pool of his own blood. She felt for a pulse; it was weak. She rolled him onto his back. "Medic, take one boot off this soldier and place it by his head. Let us move on." Maria was stern, but her chest tightened after launching the order.

"Why would we do that, Ma'am? We must take him to the wagons. I can see him breathing. He needs our help, or he will die." The medic was confused as he challenged Maria. She stared intensely into the young man's eyes. "I said take his boot off and put it by his head. Do not question my judgement or my authority. I could have you court-martialed. Do you understand?" Maria purposely raised her voice. She wanted to be heard by all around her.

"Yes Ma'am." The medic untied the soldier's left boot and placed it at his head. All triage nurses were trained in the "boot" protocol, but not the medics, not yet anyway.

"Medic, kneel down and place your ear on the soldier's chest and tell me what you hear." The medics attitude changed from challenging to fear. Placing his ear on the boy's blood-soaked uniform, he listened.

"It sounds like my father snoring during his naptime, only with a gurgle."

"And open the bottom two buttons of his shirt." Maria was training all the young medics around her. "What do you see, but more important, what do you smell?" He opened the boy's shirt, then turned away and gagged. Not only did he see bloody, obliterated organs, but he experienced a smell he never encountered.

"Medic, what you heard is not snoring, it is his lungs filling with blood. And the smell is fluid from his perforated organs seeping from his thorax. And observe the blood beginning to overflow from his mouth and nostrils."

The medic wanted to cry. "Ma'am, he is not going to live, is he?"

Maria continued to speak as she went to evaluate the next soldier. "No, he will die before we get him to the wagons. We put one boot by his head if he was alive when we left him. If those with one boot are still alive after we clear the boys we can save, we will see what we can do when we clear the dead. But the dead must be gathered quickly."

"Why quickly if they are dead?"

"Look around. In a couple of hours this field will be swarming with flies. The turkey vultures will have a feast. They are already circling in the sky above. Understand? No one wants to see their son's face half-eaten by a bird, now do they?" Joseph trained his triage nurses thoroughly. Maria did not sound like an eighteen-year-old. "Let's keep moving, boys." Maria remained cold and focused. That was the first soldier, but not the last, she would leave behind to die. The pungent smell of death filled the air as the sun rose to mid-day.

The medic apologized, but Maria paid no attention. Her father warned them when they made their decision to be a triage nurse, their personalities would be torn apart, and their hearts would never completely heal.

It was two hours since the surrender flag. Maria continued down the crest, looking for wounded soldiers. The bulk of wounded were taken to the wagons; only a few remained on the fringe. The wagons followed the nurses. Then Maria heard a soldier calling in panic just below the tree line. "Otto, where are you, Otto? Are you okay? Can you hear me, kid? Talk to me. Say something. I can't see, Otto, but I can hear you."

No, thought Maria, *it's a common name. It cannot be my Otto. It cannot be Otto Braun. Please, Lord, let it not be him*. Maria ran to the man who was yelling. Blood dripped slowly from his eyes and down his cheeks. He crawled blindly through the dirt and debris. She saw a musket ball had passed cleanly through his shoulder, and it appeared he had been struck on top of his head by a blunt object. His head wound was bleeding.

"Medic, medic!" Maria yelled as she looked at August's face. "This man has splinters in his eyes and a minor bullet wound. He can walk, so we will lead him back to the wagons on our next run."

"Who's there? You sound like a woman. What is a woman doing on the battlefield?" He did not wait for an answer; he continued to call for 'Otto'. Maria scanned the area and saw a soldier, alive, but unconscious. As she approached, she observed a tree branch had pierced his thigh, pinning him to the ground. Maria knelt next to the boy; she looked at his face.

"Oh God, no, oh my God no." Maria began to weep.

"What is it, Nurse Rothert. Is he dead? Are you okay? Why are you crying, Ma'am?" The medic was confused. This woman showed no emotion all day, and now she was in tears.

"It's my childhood friend, Otto Braun. He was drafted last week, and he is why I joined the Red Cross." Maria needed to pull herself together for everyone's sake. This was not the time to lose herself in her own human frailty.

"What is happening? Did you find my little friend Otto? We were retreating when we were hit by cannon fire. Otto, can you hear me?" August was confused.

Maria yelled, "I am a nurse here to help you both. Your Otto happens to be my best friend from home."

"Are you Maria from Cologne? He talked about you incessantly. How is he?" August wanted to help but his blindness rendered him useless, at least for the moment.

"Otto is unconscious and in shock. A tree branch punctured his thigh and pinned him to the ground. Put a tourniquet on his upper leg, medic. At the wagon will be too late." Maria knew the situation was dire. Her father explained to her this type of injury in detail when it happened to a farmer in Cologne. The farmer was trimming a tree when a branch broke loose. It severed his femoral artery; he bled out within minutes.

"Is he bleeding a lot?" asked August. "How soon can you get him stitched up? Don't worry about me. I can walk. Just let me stay with Otto."

"Nurse," asked the medic. "Should we pull the limb from his leg and get him to the wagons quickly? I think I can pull it out with little effort."

"No, no, no!" yelled Maria. "I believe the branch has pierced his femoral artery. It is the branch which keeps him alive. It is like a plug. If it slips from the artery, he will have no chance at all. We need to lift him onto a stretcher without letting the branch move. Then he must be packed tightly on his side in the wagon and the wagon must go gently back to my father for surgery."

"But how do we get the branch out of the ground without moving it?"

"We need to dig it free from under him, then we can lift him. Pull out your pocketknives."

The medics looked at Maria. "Neither of us have one. We have nothing with which to dig."

"Then we must use our hands and claw the dirt around the branch. Let's start…" Maria was interrupted.

"Don't move. Nobody moves or I'll blast this little girl's head right off." As they looked up, they saw a Hanoverian soldier with the barrel of his musket pressed firmly to the base of Maria's skull.

"Soldier, I am with the Red Cross, and according to the Geneva Treaty of…"

"Yea, yea, yea. Blah, blah, blah. My buddy got shot in the chest by one of your Prussian assholes. Save him, or I swear I'll kill this little girl of yours. I'll splatter her brains all over this field." The Hanoverian was crazed, and Maria knew it. She was terrified, but she must save Otto. She also knew she could not save him if she were dead. Her mind went in circles, evaluating scenario after scenario.

"Why don't your own doctors take care of him?"

"They said they would come back for him, but that was bullshit. He needs treatment now. That boy there onlys got a stick in his leg." The soldier's anger was intensifying, his hands were shaking. His rifle could go off at any moment.

"All right, soldier, stay calm. Take me to your friend, and I will take care of his wounds." Maria agreed with total insincerity.

"He's over that way, not far. My battalion is already back in camp, and if anybody tries to hurt you while you're saving my friend, I'll cut their throats." That was not a comforting compromise.

Maria and the medics approached the wounded soldier, the musket now between Maria's shoulder blades. "Here he is. Now save him. Take him to your wagons and back to your camp. If you don't save him, I swear to God, Nursi, I'll hunt you down and slice you up in little pieces."

"You are not going with us, soldier? Somebody needs to bring him back when he is healed."

"Little girl, they'd lock me up as a prisoner of war, and I know what you crazy Prussians do to POWs. I heard stories. You are all savages. Nope, I is staying here. Get him on that there stretcher and back to your camp, right now." The soldier watched as they put his friend on the stretcher and departed for the wagons just over the ridge. He watched until they were out of his sight, then scampered away.

"He is gone, Ma'am." They could see the wagons ahead. One of the medics looked at Maria, then down at the wounded soldier. "Nurse Rothert, remember what you taught me at the beginning?"

"What might that be, medic?" Maria's face filled with hate for this boy on the stretcher who was keeping her from saving Otto. At that moment, she did not look like a teenager. Her eyes pierced through the medic like a she-wolf planning her attack.

"I can hear this soldier's lungs gurgling and blood is coming from his mouth. You told me we must leave those who will not survive."

Maria responded indifferently. "We must clear this stretcher, medic. We have a boy with a branch in his leg who can be saved."

The medic was confused. "You mean put this Hanoverian on a wagon, then go back?"

As they spoke, two medics and a nurse passed taking a soldier to the wagons. They were puzzled when they saw a Hanoverian soldier with Maria. With head and back hunched towards the ground, Maria walked briskly to the two horsemen, one holding the surrender flag in the holster on his saddle. "One of you, give me your sword." The two looked at each other, perplexed at her request.

"Ma'am, why do you need my sword?"

"I need it."

"Ma'am, we are under a surrender flag. I thought the Red Cross was about saving lives, not killing." Maria's request was overheard by many.

They looked up from their patients as they attempted to contemplate why their head nurse needed a sword.

"Soldier, give me your sword," she demanded. The soldiers looked at each other, their eyes widened, and their shoulders shrugged. One soldier dismounted and stood by his horse. "I will escort you, Ma'am. I can help you with whatever you need to have done."

"No soldier, you must assume no responsibility for my actions. Give me your sword, no more talk. Remount and remain here." The soldier removed the sword from its sheath. Maria hurried back to her medics.

"What is she going to do with my sword?"

"You know what she is going to do. That is a Hanoverian on their stretcher. Turn your back and let her go."

Her medics had placed the stretcher on the ground just over a ridge. "Boys, turn your backs. He needs to be put out of his misery, and we need that stretcher. We all know he has no chance of survival, and we are not to treat him under the conventions of the treaty." She raised the sword. The others by the wagons could see her hands above the ridge.

"Nurse, no. Blood is spewing from the corners of his mouth. He does not have much time left. Let him die on his own. Don't do this; you will regret it." Maria was without emotion except for her passion to save Otto. At the last moment, she rammed the sword into the ground next to the soldier's neck in frustration.

"Pick him up and follow me." She grabbed one of the medics by the shirtsleeve, causing the stretcher to follow. They veered to a thorn patch where Maria gave the command, "Clear the stretcher." She grabbed one side with both hands and flipped the Hanoverian into the thorns. Wagon drivers, nurses, soldiers, and medics watched. They all felt something different about what they saw.

"Nurse Rothert, were you going to kill that soldier with the sword?"

"I am not sure, but we need it to do some digging. Let's move boys. We must save the two we are not leaving behind." By nightfall, the story would have numerous versions. She was a hero to the soldiers, but not to others.

When Maria and the medics returned they were startled. August, still bleeding from his eyes and shoulder, and his head throbbing in pain, had crawled to Otto. He dug around the branch with his pocketknife, then clawed the rest with his fingernails. The medics cut a hole in the stretcher. As they lifted Otto, Maria slid the stretcher under him. The boys lowered Otto precisely where both holes met. It was time to move. Due to the tourniquet, his leg was seeping, but not hemorrhaging. If that were to happen before the operatory, Otto would be dead within minutes.

Maria's nurses bandaged August's eyes, stitched his shoulder, and cleaned the top of his head. The two medics climbed in the wagon, holding Otto on his side, keeping him as still as possible. August insisted he remain with Otto. Maria tied a rope around his wrist and secured it to the back of the wagon gate. August spoke into the darkness which surrounded him, "Thank you, Ma'am, for saving Otto from certain death."

"That is our job, soldier. And thank you for staying by his side until we found him." She squeezed his forearm and gave him an unobserved smile.

"I could hear what was happening with the Hanoverian. I would have killed him to save all of you, but I couldn't see. I thanked the Lord when you returned safely." Even with his eyes bleeding through the bandaging, Maria could see this strong soldier weeping in gratitude.

"My name is Nurse Rothert, soldier. My father is the head surgeon back in camp." Maria was being subtle. She wanted to be sure he would know her when or if he could see again. "And what is your name?"

"August, Ma'am, August Wehmeyer. I was glad to do what I could. Will the boy be okay? He is a sweet kid, and way too young to be here." August was a rugged young man. He guarded his emotions in many ways, but he cared deeply about his family, especially his little brother. Now, he felt Otto to be part of that family.

Maria did not answer the question. Had it been anyone other than Otto, she would have left him with a boot next to his head. "He is definitely a sweet boy. We graduated from high school together last week."

"Yes, he told me, but you? I can't see your face, but your bravery is beyond your years." Maria felt an attraction to the kindness and the masculinity of this man. She was never attracted to a man his age. She only found her school chums cute. She was confused feeling something pleasant after these terrible last few hours.

Otto remained unconscious. He was placed under a scratchy woolen blanket and held motionless in the back of the wagon. Maria instructed the wagon to proceed slowly. It headed for camp.

Maria and her nurses made one final round to check on the one boot soldiers; the dead were now being gathered. Turkey vultures hopped from cadaver to cadaver. Flies swarmed the dead bodies, planting eggs in open wounds. The smell of blood and death regurgitated into the wind. The triage nurses were finished. It was time to go to Langensalza and continue treating the wounded. Few words were spoken.

Maria wanted to return before her father began surgery on Otto. She approached the horseman whose sword she borrowed. "Soldier, ride me on the back of your horse quickly to Langensalza. I need to help my father in surgery. That boy with the branch in his leg will require immediate attention. My father, Dr. Rothert, will need my assistance."

"Hop on, Ma'am." The soldier grabbed Maria by the arm and swung her onto the horse. He galloped towards camp.

The squadrons gathered the dead, placed them in canvas bags, and sowed them shut, except for their faces. They flopped them onto wagons like sacks of grain and delivered them to the train station to be identified. They would then be delivered to grieving families all over Prussia.

General Flies waited in his tent, smoking his pipe, lacking any remorse for what happened. But it would only be a few hours until his impending court-martial would be filed, relieving him of duty and stripping him of his rank.

"Wow, Aunt Carrie, that was cool. So that is how your mom and dad met? Then they got married and had you. That was a great story."

"On my child, there is more to come, a lot more."

"Does Otto die?"

"Tell you more tomorrow. Let's take a walk."

"Aunt Carrie, I don't like that General Flies man."

"He was evil, wasn't he?

13

Only God Decides When the Earth Meets the Sky.

The Battle of Langensalza
Part 2

"I could eat your pancakes everyday forever. And you put bananas in them today. That was really good. So, does Otto die and your mom and dad get married now? You promised no kissy stuff though."

"My angel, let me continue."

Maria's buttocks pounded brutally on the rump of the chestnut stallion; her thighs stung from the chafing. With her arms wrapped tightly around the horseman's waist, they galloped towards the operatory. Fifteen minutes from camp, Maria overtook the wagon transporting Otto, followed by a bedraggled August Wehmeyer stumbling over bumps and ruts in the road. The rips and tears in the knees of his pants made it obvious he had fallen many times. But he held tight to his lifeline on the wagon. As the horse slowed, Maria shouted to the medics. "What's his condition?" Her gut burned as she awaited the answer.

"He's still unconscious, but alive. He is losing blood at a steady rate and his face is cadaverous. He needs help soon, Nurse Rothert."

"I will ride ahead and have my father prepare a table for him. I will see you in fifteen." Maria clung tightly as the horseman laid boots to the stallion's sides.

Maria rode into camp and directly to the operatory. Before the horse stopped, Maria dismounted. The force of inertia caused her to stumble backward; the back of her head slammed the ground. She danced through groaning bodies on the tarpaulins of pre-op, all waiting for a chance to live another day. Nurses and medics slipped in blood as they moved soldiers in and out of surgery. Those who survived were taken to post-op. Those who did not were taken to the train station.

A clergyman knelt by the side of a soldier, "Bless this innocent soul, Lord, and accept him into your kingdom for all eternity." He sprinkled holy water on the boy, then kissed his cross and pressed it on the boys departed forehead. The men of God moved from stretcher to stretcher giving last rights to those who had an unsuccessful visit with the surgeons.

Maria, panic pulsating from her face, pulled back the tent flap of the operatory and stepped inside. "Father, Dr. Rothert, where are you? I need to speak with you immediately." Over top of the chaos, a voice boomed across the space crammed with surgical aprons.

"Nurse Rothert, remove yourself. If you wish to speak with me, do it after you have scrubbed your blood-stained hands and removed your filthy clothing. Sterile attire is being boiled outside the tent." Joseph did not look up; his eyes concentrated on removing the bullet from the young man's bowel.

Maria's face turned red with the heat of embarrassment. She knew better. She exited the tent and did what she knew was required. She removed her dress. She scrubbed the dirt and dried blood from her face, hands, and under her tightly trimmed fingernails. In haste, she darted back through screams and moans. She went to the clothesline and grabbed a damp, but sterile, surgical apron.

"Dearie, we have no dry gowns for you to wear," said an elderly woman, a sorrowful look projected from her face.

"It's OK, Ma'am. I need to return to the OR immediately!" Maria saw the wagon approaching with Otto in the back and August stumbling behind. Putting the apron overtop her long cotton underwear, she masked and reentered the operatory.

She recognizes her father despite his covered face. He was the tallest in the room even with a hunchbacked posture. He finished removing the musket ball from the young man's gut. His apron was splattered with a blend of fresh red and dried brown blood. His pants were saturated to his knees; his boots squished as he walked from table to table.

"You and your nurses did an outstanding job, Maria, and I thank God you are safe. You are uninjured, I assume." For a moment, Joseph's focus meandered to love for his daughter.

"I'm fine, Father, and thank you. I will debrief you later, but I have brought Otto back with me, and I'm afraid..."

"You mean little Otto Braun?"

"Yes sir."

"No emotions, Maria. What is your diagnosis?"

"A tree branch severed by a cannon shell fell and punctured his inner thigh..."

Joseph quickly interjected, "You didn't remove it? Tell me you didn't remove it."

"No, sir, I knew it would hemorrhage; it is still in his thigh. I placed a tourniquet above it. That is the only thing keeping him alive. He has lost a lot of blood, and he is in shock, the same as when I found him."

"Is he outside now? Take me to him when I finish here." Joseph dropped the musket ball onto the floor. "Close this boy, nurse. I must visit a soldier in pre-op." As the nurse sutured his abdomen, the ether wore off. The boy squirmed in pain. He was transferred to a stretcher and held down tightly by the medics. Morphine was injected before he left the operatory.

As Joseph and Maria exited, the wagon reached the pre-op mess of mangled bodies. "Over there, Father. He is on the wagon which has the man with the bandaged eyes stumbling behind

"What is wrong with him?" Is he a POW? You were not supposed to …"

"No, he is Prussian. He took splinters to his eyeballs at the same time Otto was pinned to the ground. He is blinded. He stayed with Otto and dug him out of the ground with his bare hands. That was what allowed us to get him on the stretcher."

"Why didn't your medics do that? They could see."

"Long story, you will hear about it around camp. Be angry with me later. They can press charges if they choose, but let's not talk now." Maria kept her focus on Otto.

Joseph looked at Maria with his eyes open wide. "Press charges on who?"

"Me, but I said we will talk later."

Joseph took control. "Medic, get the man with the bandaged eyes to post-op. Have them clean his wounds and start him on antibiotics. And tell the nurses do not, I repeat, do not attempt to remove any splinters. I will examine him later." Joseph looked at Otto; by the color of his face, he knew chances were slim. It was obvious his femoral artery was punctured; Maria was correct. And the removal of the limb would have caused him to bleed out within minutes. "Medics, bring him into the OR and keep that branch stationary." The medics removed Otto delicately from the wagon.

"Father, let me take the blind man to post-op and change his bandages."

"No, Maria, I need you at the head of my table. You must administer anesthesia. You did it for me at home, and you are good at it."

"Father, it's Otto. I can't, I just can't." Maria's emotional strength was cracking but she knew it could not, not now. She quickly changed her attitude. "Yes Father, I will do whatever you need."

"It is back to Dr. Rothert for the rest of the day. You must be strong. Remember, you volunteered because of Otto. Perhaps God has a reason for this moment. You found him and brought him back alive. Follow my instructions precisely. This will be complicated." They stared deeply into each other's eyes, then went to work.

Joseph whispered something in the ear of a lone medic. He followed the stretcher to surgery but stopped at the entrance. The two medics held the stretcher next to the table awaiting further instructions. Joseph yelled to the room, "I need two more medics." Two came running. "Here is what we must do. I will take the head of the stretcher as two of you slide your hands under the boys back. Then, Nurse Rothert will take the foot of the stretcher as the other two slide your hands under his thighs, but no one must touch the branch. Keep his body parallel to the ground. Ready, move."

They were all in position and took Otto into their arms. Medics, is he secure?"

"We have him, Doctor."

"Nurse Rothert, here we go. Let us lower the stretcher, slowly, slowly." Joseph and Maria performed with precision as the four medics held Otto parallel. When the stretcher was clear of the branch, Joseph and Maria dropped it to the floor. "Medics, place his upper body on the table." Maria moved to Otto's face and administered ether. "OK, you two holding his lower body, work your way down to his ankles. Do not let his knees bend. When I say pull, pull his legs taut. If I must use my saw, I will need leverage."

"Father, no," yelled Maria. "You can't amputate. It is Otto." Joseph ignored Maria, as did the medics following Joseph's strict instructions.

"Nurse Rothert, when I extract the branch, the femoral artery will hemorrhage. I must be quick, and you boys must hold his upper body down tightly. I will need to suture the artery if he has a chance." Maria wanted to run away, so did the medics, and so did the entire room.

"Maria, do not let him wake up, but I doubt he will. And do not get over his face or the ether will take you down. Okay, everyone ready? Here we go." Joseph looked at the medic at the door and nodded his head. He disappeared from site.

As gently as possible, Joseph pulled the branch from Otto's thigh, but as he did, blood spurted from the wound, pulsating with every heartbeat. "The artery is pierced badly." Joseph called out. "Nurse, hand me the saw. Boys, hold on tight, pull." With that, Joseph dropped to one knee and sawed with all his strength. The medics looked at the floor, unable to watch. Suddenly, one of the medics tumbled backwards onto the seat of his pants, Otto's severed leg grasped tightly in his hands.

"Nurse, sutures." As Joseph began, he observed a precarious splinter had dug its way deeply up the arterial channel towards Otto's hip. Joseph was unable to tie it off. "Now medic," he yelled to the entrance. The medic entered. "Make way people, make way, move it!" He entered with a burning log taken from the fire boiling water for the aprons. He handed it to Joseph; one end was red hot. Joseph jabbed it into the bleeding stump. A hissing sound was heard as Otto's blood attempted to extinguish the fire.

"Father, what are you doing?" Maria was not sick only because she had nothing in her stomach to vomit.

"Cauterization was the only option left." The smell of burning flesh filled the OR. Maria saw the bleeding was slowing. Otto began to move slightly. "Nurse Rothert, for God's sake, keep him under." Joseph sewed some of the smaller arteries still seeping. When he finished, he looked up. "Medics, get this boy back on the stretcher and to post-op quickly. Nurse Rothert, are you okay? Take a moment outside to clear your head of the ether, then get back in here. We are not done yet. There are boys who still need us."

Maria left the tent walking through the pool of Otto's blood. As she exited, she caught a glimpse of the medic carrying his leg, now grayish black, a putrid color she never saw before and one she would never forget. She watched as Otto's dead limb was thrown onto a fire of burning gauze, hands, and feet. She went behind the tent to dry-heaved. She thought, *it is one thing to see boys injured or dead on the battlefield. I got used to that quickly. But Otto! And my father. This is all my doing. I should have left Otto in peace with one boot at his head. I knew the rules! I knew! Oh God, let him live! This is my fault.*

Suddenly, a nurse placed her hand on Maria's back, "Nurse Rothert, Dr. Rothert says he needs you inside, and I am sorry to tell you, the boy with the leg amputation died before he reached post-op. I heard he was a friend of yours. I am so sorry."

"Thank you, nurse, but there will be time to cry later, I suppose." Maria took a deep breath.

"A lot, and for a long time, I am afraid. Will you volunteer again?"

Maria looked at her, then walked through the moaning, groaning, living, dying, soldiers on the bloody canvases to rejoin her father at the head of his table.

Alex was quiet for a while. He just stared at his Aunt Carrie. She waited until he spoke. "Aunt Carrie, I feel sick. I didn't think you could tell a story that bad, especially the part about Otto's leg. Yuk"

"My mother told me that story many times because that is the day she met my father. She told me she was never prouder of the bravery her father showed in those moments. And he was one of your grandfathers, Alex."

"I guess I'll feel proud someday, but right now, it feels a bit creepy."

"Well, that is the worst of the war part, except my mother was almost hanged for murder."

"What?"

"I will tell you that part tomorrow."

14

The Sun Rises Over the Weary But for Some, Darkness Remains

Battle of Langensalza
Part 3
June 28, 1866

"Good morning, Alex. It looks like rain today."

"I worried all night last night. Did they hang your mother? Did she die."

Carrie looked over the tops of her glasses and smiled. She continued the story.

The light of day was the only relative hint of time. Twenty-four brutal hours passed since Maria's team approached that peaceful valley and heightened emotions surged through them like a tsunami. From the first blast of cannon fire, then the sight of a war-torn battlefield, Maria finished the day as her father predicted. It was the end of her innocence and the beginning of her adulthood. His words echoed through her brain, 'You will never be the same.'

When the last soldier was taken to post-op, or the train station, Joseph and Maria removed their aprons and left the tent of horrors behind them. They took a moment to appreciate the morning breeze which cleansed the smell of death. They listened to songbirds sing in disharmony over the groans and cries emanating from post-op. Some soldiers awoke to the realization they were missing a limb. Some struggled as they were tightly strapped to their cots. The soldiers who survived without injury searched for their missing friends. If not found, they went to the train station, their faces covered with bandannas to avoid the stench of rotting flesh.

Marie turned, "May I call you Father now that we are alone?" He looked different than a week ago. He seemed to age considerably overnight, but she had not gazed into a mirror.

In bloody boots and blood-stained undergarments, they hugged. Maria began to weep. "No, no, my child. This is the time when you must be even stronger. Cry when you are alone, but not now, not even in front of me. If you wish to continue this work, this is the job. No emotions, or it will destroy you."

"Yes sir, I understand." Maria let go of her father and stood as tall as her aching body would allow. "You are a brave man, Dr. Rothert. You saved many lives today."

"We both did. And the boys you sent back were in conditions which allowed us to save many. Your decisions must have been heartbreaking, leaving some soldiers behind. That is what a triage nurse must endure within her own conscience. You must harbor no guilt towards yourself. You are wise beyond your years." Joseph had his doubts about Maria's fortitude a week ago, but no longer.

"Strangely Father, I feel no guilt, with the exception of Otto." Maria looked toward the sunrise.

"Stop, you did not cause his death, I did." Joseph reflected on his decisions in the OR.

"No Father, you will not make me feel better. It was me. I did it to both of us, and I may have caused some other boy to die while I wasted your time on Otto. I knew his femoral was punctured and he was already in shock. It was hopeless. I put you in a position of obligation." Maria turned and hugged her father again. "Oh Father, forgive me."

Joseph put space between them and looked into her eyes. "The only thing you did wrong was be human. You must not feel bad about one questionable judgement, especially when it involves a personal attachment. We all do it."

"In my heart I know that, but in the attempt to save him, I disposed of an enemy soldier. I dumped him in a patch of thorn bushes to make room for Otto." Maria turned away. "I will be punished, Father. Do you hear me? I threw a dying man away like a sack of garbage to die in the shadow of a surrender flag."

"I heard a number of versions, mainly from the officers. Two medics told me an enemy soldier had a gun barrel to the base of your skull and was going to blow your head off if you did not save his buddy. Is that true?"

"Yes, that is true."

"Would you have brought the Hanoverian back here to us if you thought we could save him? Was he treatable?"

"No Father, he would not have made it to the wagon." Maria turned and again stared into her father's eyes. "But it is one thing to leave one of our boys on the battlefield when you know he will die. It is another to toss a man into thorn bushes and leave him for dead."

"It is war. You did what you needed to do. If you had refused to take him on the stretcher, your brains would be all over that field. Do you know what that would have done to the infancy of the Red Cross? Women would be terrified to volunteer." Joseph sighed in relief. "And the way the story goes, you are a hero among the men, putting our soldiers first."

"Really Father, they feel that way?" Maria had a confused smile on her face, somewhere between pride and concern.

"But some soldiers, and most of the townspeople in the wagons, say you killed him with a sword. They say you stabbed him through the chest before you threw him in the bushes. That is the other version. Let us not share any of this with the Brauns. Otto fought with valor, and during the battle, a branch from a cannon shell severed his femoral artery. That is what happened."

"Thank you, Father. And I did not stab the man. I thought about it, and I wanted to, but he was alive, though barely, when I tossed him. I think I will clean up, and I need something to eat."

"I will join you, and we can rest for a few hours. I am famished."

"First, I wish to check on the blind man who helped Otto. I want to thank him for digging him out to get the stretcher under him. To do that while his eyes bleed was gallant. He heard the Hanoverian take me away. That is when he crawled over and started digging. It was heroic."

"Maria, I wish to go with you, but not now. We must rest. When we awaken, we will check on all the boys in post-op. We must watch their wounds carefully. One in four will die from infection, most by week's end."

"Father, there is something about that blind soldier. I must know why he was loyal to Otto. Maybe he is from Cologne. I hope so."

Joseph sensed excitement in Maria's voice. "Be careful, my dear, it sounds as if you are taking a fancy to this soldier of whom you know nothing."

Maria blushed. "Father, really, I am a nurse. I respect the man, that is all." Joseph nodded. Let's make him our first visit when we return." Joseph smiled.

Joseph and Maria were the last of the surgical team to reach the village. Although the dusty road was only at a slight incline, the fatigue on their knees and ankles was agonizing. As they walked, their blood-filled boots squished like children caught in a rainstorm.

On the side of the church, buckets of water were furnished by the townspeople. Behind sheets on clotheslines, the naked nurses scrubbed themselves in the crisp morning breeze. Pointed utensils dug human skin and dried blood from under their toe and fingernails. The villagers wrapped them in warm clean towels and blankets. They were a gift from God.

As Maria concentrated on her own hygiene, the nurse next to her asked, "You think they will get you for what you did?"

Maria looked up. "I'm sorry, get me for what?"

"For murdering that enemy soldier."

"I didn't murder anybody. What do you mean?"

"I was there. I saw you stab him. We all did. But I won't say anything, I promise. After what I saw, I wanted to kill some Hanoverians as well. We are not supposed to treat the enemy, but I am sure we are not supposed to kill them either, especially under a surrender flag." The nurse was not condescending, just factual. "You breached the Red Cross articles by putting him on your stretcher in the first place, not to mention the international rules of war by killing him."

"I told you, I didn't kill him, but I did what I had to do to save one of ours. Hand me the soap." Maria wanted to go into detail, but she was too tired, and the trauma of the last day made her callous. She knew she must speak only to her father from here on.

As she finished cleaning herself, a middle-aged woman resembling everyone's grandmother, placed a woolen blanket over her shoulders and gave her a damp, but clean, uniform. The uniform exhibited shadows of unremovable bloodstain. "Come child, come inside the church and I will get you something to eat. Then I will take you to my house so you may rest."

Maria wanted to weep. This kind woman pulled her from a world of violent rancor and back into the world of peace and kindness. "Thank you so much, Ma'am. Food and a place to lay my head for a few hours is so appreciated. Where might you live?"

"See the small cottage down the road with the thatched roof and the swing on the porch? My husband and I live there. Just go there when you are finished. He and I discussed it."

"Discussed what?"

"Since our children are grown and gone, we are not afraid to have you in our home." The woman gave a patronizing smile.

"Why would you be afraid to have me in your home?"

"We heard you are the nurse who went crazy and stabbed the Hanoverian boy. You rammed the blade right through his chest, I am told. You are the one, aren't you missy?" Maria frowned with surprise. "You certainly don't look like you could kill somebody like a savage. Pray hard and often, young lady, and the Lord may someday forgive you for your mortal sin. People do funny things in crazy situations, I guess. The people in town with children feel danger in your presence." The woman took Maria's hand in sympathy.

Maria went from confused to shocked. *Everyone has heard. But I did not stab him. Wait, oh my, I did raise the sword and stick it in the ground out of frustration. They are all coming after me. I did what was right, and I thought the army agreed. I must talk to Father.*

Nausea invaded Maria. She went from feeling glorified on the battlefield to being a war criminal. She entered the church where her father was eating a plate of venison, sauerkraut, and drinking a hot cup of coffee.

"You look and smell a lot better, Maria. This food is delicious. These country people know how to cook. Have a seat." Joseph's weariness was pronounced by the bags under his eyes and his haggard posture. His face was chafed and rosy from heavy scrubbing. "Maria, is something wrong? It looks as if you've seen a ghost. My dear, you did everything you could for everyone, especially Otto."

"Two people, one nurse and one elderly townswoman, think I murdered that Hanoverian in the field. The woman told me the townspeople are afraid to have me in their homes and around their children. Father, I was forced at gunpoint to put him on my stretcher, and he was never going to live. It was either him or Otto on that stretcher. Father, I dumped him, but I didn't kill him." Maria sat on the bench and began to cry behind the palms of her hands.

"Maria, I was told there will be an inquiry. The soldiers see you as a hero, not a criminal. You threw away an enemy to save one of their own. The townspeople are not soldiers. If you would have brought that boy back, I would not have operated on him."

"You mean, you would have let him die on his own outside the OR?"

"It's the treaty and no one would have questioned it." Joseph patted Maria's knee under the table. "Let's go over exactly what happened but do it away from the others."

Maria told the story once again, but in great detail. At the end, she finished with something Joseph did not expect.

"Father, I graduated from high school only two weeks ago and the most violent thing I ever saw was a dog fight in the alley. In the last twenty-four hours, I heard cannons and gunfire. I saw pain, blood, and death. I heard boys screaming in agony. I watched my best friend die as my father amputated his leg."

"Yes, Maria, and you have handled it well."

"Father, when I went back to the stretcher with the sword, I was going to thrust the tip of that blade into his throat as hard as I could. I wanted him dead. I was angry. He and his buddy were keeping me from saving Otto. I could imagine the feeling of the blade puncturing his throat and I enjoyed it."

"But you restrained."

"Only because the medic brought sanity back to me. I was insane, Father."

"But you didn't do it. What are you saying?"

"When I recall the moment, I can see his face vividly. I didn't care if he had a family or friends. I didn't even think about it."

"But now you feel guilty for leaving him to die."

"No, not at all. What I am trying to say is, I wish I would have stabbed him. He was the enemy. His army shot and maimed all those boys I treated and those I had to let die. I felt strong when I flipped that stretcher. I have no remorse for feeling that way, none. Am I evil? Have I always had an evil side?"

"No, you did what needed to be done to save a life. But it became personal for you. That was unfortunate. What you did was an act of love for Otto. All of us, both sides, have been thrust into this situation by the greed of the leaders of Prussia and Austria. They lust for power over one another. And when they unite as one nation, they will go after the rest of Europe. We are an aggressive people. It is our Germanic culture. Soldiers are tools. They do what they are told, or they are locked in the brig, or shot for treason."

Joseph looked around, then kissed Maria on the forehead. "Get some rest. All will be fine. We must visit the blind man soon."

Maria forced a smile.

Maria Visits August
Joseph Has a Reason
to Make the Young Man's Acquaintance

Battle of Langensalza
Part 4
June 28, 1866

The weary staff rested as the morning flipped to afternoon. Joseph and Maria splashed water onto their faces and drank a strong cup of coffee. They limped to the post-op on tired, aching legs. Humidity accentuated the musty smell of the canvas around them. They entered the tent to the droning sounds of pain and the pungent aroma of sterility. Nurses moved from patient to patient checking for signs of infection. The clergymen continued to pray for a soldier's recovery or delivered to them their last rites.

"Where is this young man, Maria? Are you sure you will recognize him?"

"His eyes will be bandaged, Father, I mean Doctor Rothert. His head wound will be wrapped, and his arm will be in a sling." Maria scanned rows after row of cots.

The Great Great Aunts from Prussia

"You didn't tell me of his head and shoulder. You let that man walk back with a head trauma? I do not understand, Maria. You know better."

"He insisted he stay with Otto, and we had no room for him on the wagon. I explained to him he could ride on another one, but he was dedicated to our friend. So, I tied him to the gate." Maria stopped. "There he is, over there in the corner." She moved through the maze. Joseph followed slowly.

Maria was unsure if August was awake, asleep, or dead. Joseph felt for a pulse while Maria placed the back of her hand on his cheek to feel for fever. His cheek was a normal temperature, and his skin was the color of life. Then, August's body jerked as he emerged from a deep sleep. "Who's there? Where am I? Am I captured? Where am I? Who is touching me?"

Maria spoke softly, "You are safe and in your Prussian camp, soldier. Your injuries have you in post-op."

"You are the nurse who saved Otto and tied me to the wagon, are you not? I recognize your voice. But it is much more serene. All I heard on the field was you barking orders like a drill sergeant." Joseph smiled; Maria rolled her eyes. August was surprisingly alert.

"Yes, that was me. My name is Nurse Rothert. How are you feeling? Are you in much pain?" Maria knelt by his bedside and put her hand on top of August's.

"Who is the man with you? The one with the rough hands feeling my pulse. Is he a doctor?" Although taking a sharp blow to the head, August was coherent, his memory was accurate.

"That is Doctor Rothert. He is the head surgeon in camp. We both came to check on you. We are curious why you were so dedicated to our Otto."

"Are you Otto's parents?" August continued without hesitation, leaving no room for an answer. "I met him the day before the battle. Fine young boy you have. He was wandering the camp aimlessly, like a

99

lost puppy. He couldn't find his squadron. I took him under my wing. They gave him no training at all. I had to teach him how to load and fire his weapon."

"But why did you do that?" asked Maria.

"He reminded me of my little brother back in Berlin." Maria's heart dropped a notch discovering August did not live in Cologne.

Joseph needed some facts for Maria's upcoming inquiry. "So, you were retreating when the cannon shell exploded. That was before the surrender?"

"At the same time. We were retreating to the crest of the hill. When I looked back, the Hanoverians were invading the valley on horseback. I saw our soldiers in the valley dropping to their knees, their hands behind their heads. That is when the first shell exploded. I hit the dirt. I felt horses vibrating the ground. I called for Otto to drop his rifle. That is when I saw him pinned to the ground. Not thinking, I took off to help him with my rifle still in my hand. Then another shell exploded in the trees and splinters pierced my eyes. A few seconds later, I felt a bullet pass through my shoulder, and I was hit on the head and knocked unconscious. When I came to I called to Otto, but he did not answer. Then I heard a woman's voice. I thought I was in heaven except that she was barking orders."

"It sounds terrible," said Joseph. "You are a brave man."

"Sir, whoever gave the order to attack was uninformed as to our preparedness. And somehow, they knew we were coming. With all these young boys flooding in the last few days, they knew they had to be untrained. Their spies blended right into our confusion." August was overstepping the boundaries of loyalty, but he didn't care. His head ached, his shoulder ached, and he was blind. His face grimaced in pain.

"Son, have you received morphine lately?"

"No sir, I refused. I heard I can become addicted. I would rather hurt for a while."

Joseph got the attention of a nurse. She returned and handed him a syringe. "Son, your wounds are not life threatening, however you will need something for your pain. We will make sure you do not become addicted. But we need to talk more before I inject you."

"Thank you, sir. What do you need from me?" Joseph needed a witness to yesterday's events, even though he was not an eyewitness.

"So, you both were wounded while the battle was still being fought."

"I must say yes, sir. Otto and I were retreating when the canon shells exploded. And I was shot because I still had my rifle in my hand."

"What do you remember after you heard Nurse Rothert's voice?"

"I heard her giving the medics orders, but then I heard a soldier with a Hanoverian accent threaten to kill your wife if she didn't treat his friend. Shoot her in the head, he said."

August continued his recount. It was the same as Maria's.

"When can I visit your son, Doctor? He must be tired and weak. Maria injected August with morphine. She looked at her father, neither wanted to say it.

"First off, Nurse Rothert is my daughter, not my wife. Secondly, we did refer to him as 'our Otto,' but he was our pastor's son back in Cologne."

"Was? Did you say Otto was your pastor's son? Do you mean he's dead? No, he was just a kid. He was a kind boy. Wilhelm and Bismarck had no right to pull those boys from their innocent lives and bring them here to die. We walked into a trap, sir. They were waiting for us. And because of that, Otto is gone?" Maria saw the bandages over August's eyes turning pink from the mixture of blood and tears.

Joseph spoke, "August, I will not repeat this, and I will deny I ever said it. It was not Bismarck's orders. General Flies was to block the Hanoverians and force them in the direction of our main divisions. He deliberately disobeyed orders. It cost Otto, and many others, their lives. It was an act of ego and arrogance. He will be treated harshly, I assure you."

101

"Not harshly enough. I will kill him myself if I get the chance." Maria held August down by the shoulders. He grimaced in pain.

"I would help you if I thought we could get away with it, but let's not do that. I want us both to live long and happy lives."

Maria understood August's rage. His anger was justified. "Soldier, allow me to remove your bandages so Dr. Rothert can evaluate the damage to your eyes. He will determine if he can remove the splinters surgically. You must remain calm. And we are still unsure how severe your concussion may be until we see your pupils." Maria removed the bandages.

"Son, how many fingers do you see?" asked Joseph.

"I don't know Doctor; everything is a blur." August was calm.

"Can you see colors?"

"I only see brown and white. What does that mean?"

"It means those are the only colors in here. It was a useless question on my part. I am sorry." Joseph squeezed August's good shoulder. "Let's go outside in the sunlight where I can get a better look at your eyeballs." They took August outside and returned.

"Can you fix my eyes, sir?"

"I don't know, but I will do what I can. You do not have a concussion from the bump on your head, and your shoulder should heal nicely, but you will need to endure some pain for a while, perhaps a few months. Nurse Rothert will clean and redress your wounds. Get some rest." Joseph had no experience with eyes, and he knew only one eye surgeon, unfortunately, he resided in America.

"Thank you, Doctor," August slurred gently. The morphine was taking effect.

Joseph walked away as Maria rebandaged. She touched August's face with her soft and caring hand. "August, thank you for your dedication to my friend. I will always care about you for that." Maria smiled. August could not see her expression, but he could feel it in the tone of her voice.

"And thank you, Nurse. I heard you did something to an enemy soldier so you could help us save Otto."

"Soldier, I…"

"Please, call me August, August Wehmeyer. Will you come back and talk to me sometime and help me write a letter to my parents?"

"I would love to help you write a letter to your parents. And you must call me Nurse Rothert when others are around, but when we are alone, call me Maria. No, forget that. Call me Maria anytime." She stroked August's forearm. He smiled as she returned him to the darkness; his pain was receding, and his heart was grinning.

16

Maria Feels a Tightening Around Her Neck

Battle of Langensalza
Finale

"Maria, awaken my child." Joseph gently stroked her soft, messy hair.

Her eyes fluttered as she attempted to regain awareness from her nap. She sat on the edge of her bed, not knowing exactly where she was or what time it might be. Joseph opened the curtains to let the late afternoon sunlight assist in her emergence. "What is it, Father?"

"We have been summoned to a tribunal headed by Lieutenant Otterbein. We are to come immediately." Maria could see concern on her father's face; she heard nervousness in his voice.

"What time is it, Father, and who is Lieutenant Otterbein?"

"It's not important. Get dressed, comb your hair, and make yourself presentable."

As they left the humble home of the elderly couple, Maria noticed the husband sitting in a rocking chair staring at her. He had his hunting rifle on his lap. They walked down the dirt road, past the post-op, and towards the center of camp. Two guards intercepted them; they escorted them to the command tent. Outside, Maria noticed a body lying on a barren patch of ground, covered by a sheet; the sheet was spotted with blood. Flies swarmed the corpse, attempting to penetrate to the body beneath. The familiar waft of death floated on the breeze. As Maria and Joseph entered the tent, they saw two officers and one of Joseph's surgeons positioned at a long table in front. Attending the hearing as well were Maria's two medics, the horseman who gave her his sword, and a townsman. It was obvious what was happening, and it was what Joseph expected.

"Will Maria and Joseph Rothert please come forward," said the lieutenant. They stood in front of the officer. "Are you Maria Rothert of the Red Cross?"

"Yes sir." She was shaking.

"And are you Captain Joseph Rothert, the head surgeon in camp?"

"Yes sir." Joseph radiated confidence.

"The townsman sitting among us came to me this morning. He felt an obligation to God and his country to inform me of a heinous act of murder by one of your nurses, Dr. Rothert. He told me he watched Maria Rothert demand a sword from a horseman, go over a ridge, raise the sword above her head and thrust it into a Hanoverian soldier, killing him instantly. He then saw her and two medics throw the dead body into a patch of thorn bushes."

Maria began to speak but was interrupted by the lieutenant.

"First, let me start by saying, I am against this idea of women on a battlefield. Women are unable to control their emotions, and it did not take long to prove my theory." The lieutenant continued. "Nurse Rothert, we are here to determine whether you committed an act of murder and, if so, you will be punished as a war criminal. Do you understand the gravity of the situation? If found guilty, the punishment for this offense is either life in prison, or you will be hanged by the neck until dead."

Shock swept through Maria; her legs weakened. Joseph held her under her arm. But the possibility of his daughter being executed was almost more than he could bear as well, but somehow he retained his composure.

"Lieutenant, I assume you are referring to the death of a Hanoverian soldier on the battlefield," Joseph replied.

"No sir, I refer to the Hanoverian soldier murdered under a white flag of surrender by Nurse Rothert." The lieutenant made it clear what direction this hearing would take.

"Nurse Rothert followed my succinct orders, sir, the same orders I gave all my triage nurses when we arrived in Langensalza. They all followed my orders perfectly and saved many lives by leaving those incapable of survival behind." The committee members listened intently.

"Dr. Rothert, this is a simple question of yes or no. Did you instruct your nurses in the field to stab an enemy to death under a flag of surrender?" The lieutenant had guilty already in his head, but unaware of the perilous situation he was approaching.

"Of course not, Lieutenant, that is an inane accusation. Do you agree a soldier with no chance of survival, with or without surgery, should be brought to my medical team and given priority over those we can save?" Joseph stared viciously at the lieutenant.

"Who gave you the authority to play God, Doctor Rothert. Who gave you permission to implement that policy? General Flies could be held responsible for your immoral decisions."

"First of all, General Flies has more to worry about than my morality, but the answer to your question is Otto Von Bismarck. He is your villain, sir. It is his policy." The lieutenant was puzzled by Joseph's answer. So puzzled, he became short of breath.

"I must see those procedures in writing, Doctor. I don't believe you. You are saying you personally communicate with Von Bismarck? Don't complicate this case with your lying under oath."

"Why do you think I am here at the first battle in which Red Cross nurses have participated? Von Bismarck sent me to the American Civil War to study wartime medicine and communication tactics. I wrote the Red Cross training manuals which he approved. I can deliver …"

"No, no, Doctor, I believe you for now." The Leutenant changed directions quickly. "How was Nurse Rothert sure the Hanoverian was incapable of survival, and if so why did she run him through with a sword?"

"I assume that is the body outside under the sheet?"

"Yes, with the help of the townsman over there, our soldiers retrieved it from the bush of thorns." The lieutenant looked at the doctor sitting next to him. "Would you and Dr. Rothert go outside and exam his wounds, then report your findings to the court."

The doctors left and returned quickly. "What are your findings doctors. Joseph stayed silent. "It appears the wound in his chest is from a bullet perforating his lower lung and splintering his rib cage. His mouth was still filled with blood and his cheeks were covered where his lungs overflowed."

"So, you are saying the soldier was not savable, doctor? Do you both agree as well, Doctor Rothert,? The soldier had no chance of survival?"

"Without a doubt, sir. I agree completely."

"Nurse Rothert, treating the enemy is against the Red Cross charter, am I correct? And if he was going to die anyway, why put him on your stretcher, then murder him? None of this is making sense."

With that, Maria's medics rose to their feet and asked permission to speak. The lieutenant granted their request. The medics relayed to the court in detail the events leading to the encounter with the Hanoverian. The lieutenant was almost convinced he had no case.

"Medic, I have one final question which is unclear. If Nurse Rothert was sure the Hanoverian was going to die, why did she run him through with a sword?"

"She didn't. She…"

Hearing that, the townsman stood yelling with ire. He pointed his finger at Maria. "Liar, liar, those boys are liars. I don't know what is going on here, but I saw you do it, little girl. I was driving my wagon in that field. I saw you get the sword from that horseman over there and run back to your medics. I saw you raise the blade above your head, and with both hands, mind ya, you ram it into that boy's throat. I saw you do it. I don't care if he was the enemy and I don't care if he was gonna die, that is just wrong in the eyes of God."

The lieutenant looked at Joseph's colleague. "Doctor, did you see a stab wound on the corpse in the throat or upper chest area?"

"No sir."

"And you, horseman, when she returned your sword, was there blood on the blade?"

"No sir, just mud."

"Townsman, you say she stabbed him in the throat, but there is no sign of a stabbing. Nurse Rothert, what did the townsman see?"

"Lieutenant, my medics were over a small ridge with the stretcher on the ground. He could have only seen the tops of our heads."

"Townsman, is that true?"

"Well, yes sir. But she thrust the sword violently into the soldier from where I stood." That was enough from the townsman.

"But Nurse Rothert, why did you need the sword?"

"As my medics told you, we needed it to dig."

"So, what did the townsman see?"

"Sir, my emotions ran high in that moment. When I had the sword in my hand, I saw the Hanoverian as the obstacle keeping me from saving our boys. I was livid. I raised the sword, but my medic stopped me. I owe him my life. I came down hard and stuck the sword in the ground out of frustration." Maria ended her plea.

The lieutenant heard all he needed, especially after Von Bismarck's name was introduced. "I think we all find Nurse Rothert did her duty in saving our soldiers' lives by putting them first. The death of the

Hanoverian was inevitable. But before we finish, Nurse Rothert, I am told you and your nurses did an outstanding job, and all of Prussia can be proud. But remember, war has its own rules; many are broken, and young men die. You came close to crossing that line. Follow the rules even though your heart may tell you differently."

"Thank you, sir." Maria wanted to cry as Joseph hugged her, but as taught, she held back.

As he finished, the lieutenant was handed a telegram. It was short. "People, hold your position. Doctor Rothert, you and your staff must head to Bohemia day after tomorrow. Compared to what is coming in Bohemia, I am told this battle was child's play. I am to inform you more Red Cross volunteers will join you. You must begin their training as soon as you arrive. All right, people, let's move; we have a war to fight." Word spread through camp as to Maria's innocence, and of Joseph's importance to Von Bismarck. They were both treated as royalty.

"Father, I am having second thoughts about this."

"About what, Maria?"

"In the last week I have seen death, blood, and guts where I used to see pastoral landscapes. I dumped a man in a thorn bush and left him to die. I lost my best friend as I watched you saw off his leg. And was almost executed for murder. I must say, I am frightened." Maria's lips tightened as she stared into her father's wise countenance.

"Maria, you made the decision to come here; it was all you. And you made the decision to become a triage nurse; no one else. I warned you; you would never be the same. You have been courageous and learned to place life in the highest regard. We would not have saved half of those boys without you and your nurses." Joseph was proud. "Maria, courage is bred from fear. Stay on this path and you will be an influence on many people for generations to come."

"Father, I have feelings I never experienced before, most are loving, but not all. I want to continue, but the court-martial could happen again. That is what scares me."

"Maria, do as I instruct and follow my orders. Von Bismarck will not allow any of these hot-shot officers to challenge you or any of our people." Maria smiled. She now knew her father possessed power, and she was proud of his humility.

"Is that all you need of me, sir?" Maria began to walk away, but Joseph grabbed her by the arm and whispered in her ear.

"One more thing. Be sure you get the blind soldier's full name and address so you can write to him in Berlin when we get home." Maria blushed.

"Father, I don't really know him. What if he doesn't wish to give it to me?" Maria looked at the ground.

"Tell him I have contacts which might be able to help his vision when the war is over. Will that make it easier?" Maria looked up and finally smiled.

"Do you really have contacts, Father? That would be wonderful. I will give him our address as well." Maria's emotions in the last hour soared and dove like a hawk flying through the mountains.

"Maria, I want to help him for what he did for Otto, and…" Joseph hesitated.

"And what Father?"

"I want him to see how beautiful you are, since both of you already have feelings for each other. I like the boy, Maria. I don't know why, but I do." Joseph kissed his daughter on the forehead.

"Father, really." Maria turned and walked away, hiding a girlish smirk on her face. After all, she was only eighteen.

"Wow, Aunt Carrie. That was your mother and your grandpa in that war. You must be so proud. And now I am proud of them, too. But did your father ever get to see how pretty your mother was."

"There is more to the story if you want to hear. My father became a famous man."

"So, he did see again. That's great."

"No, I didn't say that. My father was blind for the rest of his life."

"Then how could he get famous?"

"I guess you want me to tell you more?"

"Yes!"

17

Carrie Takes Alex Back to Post-War Berlin

**The Courtyard
of the Wehmeyer Home
Berlin, Prussia
September 15, 1866**

"Good morning Alex. I heard the adoption agency's approval came through and you are going to have a baby sister. That is exciting."

"Yea, we are all excited, but it wasn't easy, Aunt Carrie. The adoption lady thought I was kinda weird at first, but some child psycostisis, or something like that, said I was sort of normal." Carrie smiled at Alex's innocence. "I want to hear about your father and how he got famous even though he couldn't see. You started off the story with him in a garden. What did he do that made him so famous? Tell me, Aunt Carrie, I want to know."

"Alex Beckham, that would be way too easy. You like my storytelling, do you not? I think someday you will be a good storyteller, maybe even write a book or two."

"I hope so, that would be really fun."

"You remember August's little brother pestering him in the garden?"
"I do."
"Then let's go back and pick up where we left off."

After the confrontation with August's little brother, Henry, and his mother, he sat silently on the concrete bench in the courtyard. He had the latest letter from Maria gripped tightly in his hand. His mind regressed to that horrible day in Langensalza only three months prior. His chest continued to heave in anger; chills of adrenaline rushed through his body. His anxiety was reaching a breaking point. His physical pain, his depression over Otto, and the loss of his sight spilled into negative actions toward his family. But with the intimate letters from Maria arriving weekly, there was a duality in his heart. He looked forward to her expressions of fondness, and her genuine respect. But then he envisioned himself as the blind man on the street corner with a tin cup. The question haunted him. *Why would any woman as wonderful as Maria want me for a husband?*

Then he heard a gentle voice. "August, it's Katarina. Are you okay, my love?" His twin sister approached. She kissed him on the cheek below his bandaged eyes; her mere presence caused serenity.

"I know it's you, Katarina. I heard you speaking with Mother, and you always wear the ambrosial perfume I gave you for your birthday." August's emotions settled like the light rain at the end of a summer storm.

Katarina gently hugged August's bandaged face; she kissed the scar on top of his head. "Mother is quite upset with herself, and so is Henry, because of their lack of compassion for you. What happened to make you so angry?"

"Leave it alone, and I want no sympathy from them." August handed Katerina the letter he gripped in his hand.

"Another letter from Maria? You are afraid, aren't you?"

"Would you not be? I am a blind man. I may never see again. I may never read again. I will never be an educated aristocrat like her and her family. All I can do in my life is throw pottery, or should I say, all I might be able to do is throw pottery." August cried into Katerina's embrace. She was the only person to whom he revealed his vulnerability.

"Have you tried yet, throwing pottery I mean? Have you asked Father to let you try at his factory? Where is this fear coming from, my twin? You are the bravest man I know. Why do you do this to yourself? Pull it together and have faith. It appears the nurse from Cologne has faith in you. She knows you are blind, and she keeps writing." Katerina and August were close, but until now, she always needed him more than he needed her.

"I will ask father to give me a chance. Although still panful, my shoulder is strengthening, perhaps next week." August was trying, but not with confidence.

"Shall we take a walk to the park and read the letter, or we can do it in your room. You decide, August." The others knew of the letters, but only Katerina knew details; she swore secrecy. And if one of Maria's letters said goodbye, he wanted Katarina to be there when it happened.

"If we go to my room, Mother will know it is you reading the letters. But if we go to the park…"

"August, she knows. She asks me all the time about them; who are they from, what do they say? I tell her I respect your privacy. She is nosey, but she is our mother."

"I love you, Katerina. Let's go to the park. It feels wonderful out here, and the smell of the turning leaves is so sweet." Katarina took August by the hand and led him out the gate, but he stopped.

"Katarina, run back and tell Mother I am sorry. And tell her not to tell Father what Henry did this afternoon. I don't want him to be punished. He is a kid; I forget that sometimes. I think he looks up to me like I am a war hero. It must hurt him to see me like this, weak and frail."

"August Wehmeyer, you are a war hero; you are our hero in every way. We all look up to you. You will be back to full strength shortly." She ran to the kitchen and returned promptly. "Done." She took him by the hand, and they left the courtyard, the letter clenched in Katerina's hand. She loved reading Maria's letters, as much as August loved hearing them. She dreamed of the day when she would write love letters to a beau.

18

Letters from Maria Rothert
After the End of the Austro-Prussian War
July 31, 1866

Letter received August 4, 1866

Dear August,

 The war is over. Father and I are home safe. Even though it was only a three-week war, the fighting was fierce. I was unable to contact you until now. I must ask with most sincerity, please respond to this letter as soon as possible. I am unable to rest until I know your condition. I pray you are well. Over half of the boys we treated in those three battles died of infection. We are concerned about you. Father and I will never forget the day we met. Otto's family wishes to thank you for your dedication to their son. Although we could not attend, the funeral service was terribly sad. I am told you were named specifically in the eulogy. The congregation mentioned you in their prayers.

 Although I have a lot to share, I must know of your health right away. Please send me a telegram. Father and I anxiously await your response.

My affections and respect,
Maria Rothert

Letter received August 12, 1866

Dear August,

Father and I received your telegram. We are so relieved you are healing and regaining your strength. I am sorry you have not recovered your sight. Father assures me a brave man such as yourself will not allow a handicap to keep him from love, success, and a happy life.

When returning from the battlefield in late July, my family wept in happiness for our safe return. We slept for three days and ate anything and everything our housekeeper prepared.

My mind, however, cannot rid itself of the haunting sights and the rancid smells of war. No matter how hard I try, my mind will not allow me to remove all the blood from under my fingernails and toenails.

If you wish, please write back. I would love to hear about your family and your plans to restart your life. I am so happy you are safe and healthy. I would be most pleased to see you someday soon.

To my hero,
Maria Rothert

Letter received September 1, 1866

Dear August,

I so enjoy your letters and learning about your family and friends. Your writing skills are beautiful and poetic; a talent I did not expect. I hope I have not overloaded you with information about myself. I am getting to a point where I believe I know you better than most of my friends in Cologne. Since my return, I find conversations with them to be rather juvenile.

Father has been meeting with Von Bismarck in Berlin. He has been offered a position as a surgical professor in Berlin, but our family is strongly rooted in Cologne. His practice is here, as well as his dedication to the stability of our family.

He will spend some time teaching at Charite Medical College in Berlin. Von Bismarck also wants him to return to the United States and study the latest in surgical techniques at the Harvard Medical School.

He says he would like to visit and talk with you on his next journey to Berlin. Would you be so gracious as to welcome a visit from him, if nothing more than to allow him the opportunity to thank you for your protection of Otto?

Write back soon. I live for your letters.

To my sweet friend. I adore you.

Maria Rothert

"So, how many letters did she write. I really don't want to hear a bunch of mushy ones."

"No Alex, she only writes one more."

"What do you mean one more. I thought they got married. Tell me she didn't tell him good-bye. How could she only write one more? I am confused."

"Do you want me to continue?"

"Yes, keep going, Aunt Carrie" Carrie loved playing with his curiosity.

19

Maria's Last Letter

Berlin, Prussia
September 15, 1866

Katarina and August made their way to the park with Maria's most recent correspondence. It was an early autumn this year. They were surrounded by wilting flowers and multi-hued leaves which August could not see. He felt a soft breeze on the legs of his trousers. He heard the crackling of decaying leaves blowing over his shoe tops. Katarina sat him on a marble bench near a fountain. A soft mist touched her brother's cheek.

"All right, are you ready for this most recent letter from Maria? I have read all her letters, and I assure you this will not tell you goodbye. She loves you, August. Any woman hears it in her words. But how could any woman love a man who put a dead mouse in his twin sister's slipper?" Katarina placed her hand on top of August's and giggled.

"Okay, funny girl, get on with it. If it is unwelcomed news, I am thankful you will be unable to see my tears through my bandages." August handed her the letter.

Letter received September 16, 1866
(The letter which caused the problem in the garden with Henry)

Dear August,

    I have something I must tell you. I pray you find it reasonable and not offensive. [Katrina looked at August; his hands clenched tightly together between his knees.] I made you aware Father took a part-time professorship at Charite in Berlin. To do so, he must travel to the United States for three months to learn new surgical and sterilization technics at the Harvard School of Medicine. One of his studies will be eye surgery and the removal of foreign bodies. It is experimental. He made a request to Von Bismarck to take you with him in an attempt to restore your eyesight. The request was granted. It is now your decision. Father will visit you and your family in the next few days to discuss this opportunity. He is in Berlin now. There is no need to respond. By the time I receive your answer, he will have returned.

    I will not share details. He will do that in person with you and your family. My father has respected you and supported our friendship from the day he met you in the post-op. He is a good man. Please listen to his proposal.

To my loving soldier,
Maria Rothert

    Katarina and August sat in silence. The thought of someone cutting on his eyes was more than uncomfortable; it was terrifying. "Has this been a trick the entire time, Katarina, to use me as a research animal? I cannot believe she would do this to me."

    "Shame on you, August Wehmeyer. I should turn you over my knee and spank you. I understand your fear, it seems natural to me. But Maria and her father are not using you. They love you; they respect you. Perhaps this is God's way of rewarding your compassion to that young boy, Otto. Please, be open to what the doctor has to say. We will help you, but this is your decision, and yours alone." Katarina was frightened and a bit skeptical as well. "Let's go back to the house. It is almost dinnertime. Father will be home soon."

Katarina kissed August on the forehead and took him by the hand. They returned home. Katarina changed the bandages on his eyes, but before they joined the family table, she stopped.

"August, let us think this through before we tell Mother and Father. Find out if you can function in Father's pottery factory before you risk surgery."

"Yes Katerina, tonight I will ask Father to give me a run at turning the wheel once again, but this time as a blind man." Katrina squeezed his hand and with her unseen smile led him to his chair for the family's evening meal.

Dinner concluded and the children helped Hilda clear the table; August and his father sat alone. "Father, I must inform you of something, and also make a request."

"No son, I am not going to take Henry to the shed, although I thought about it when I learned of what he did. I know you did not want me to know, but your mother and I keep no secrets. As hard as it may be to understand, Henry wants things to return to the way they were. He is confused; give him time. He will learn to respect your courage even more as time goes on."

"Thank you, Father, I understand this is hard on everyone. But warn him; I will knock him on his ass if he hits my shoulder again. It is stronger, but it is still painful to a slap."

James laughed. "Agreed, he must be taught the consequences of his actions. And I told your mother to respect your privacy. If you have a relationship you wish to keep secret, it is up to you." James lit his pipe and stirred his coffee. "So, what do you want to tell me, August?"

August informed his father of an impending visit by Dr. Rothert but stopped there. Then he made his request. "Father, I see nothing but a blur, and I may never see anything more. Will you give me a chance to turn the potter's wheel at your factory, like I did as a teen? I want to know if I can feel my way to competency. I love the feel of raw clay in my hands and the earthy smell."

"Without a doubt, son. I have waited for your desire to be functional. I knew it would comeback." James got up and gave his son a proud hug, but as he did, a knock came at the front door. With Hilda and the children unable to hear over the clanking of glasses and dishes, James answered.

A tall man dressed in tails and a top hat stood on the stoop. His demeanor was intimidating.

"Are you Mr. Wehmeyer, father of August Wehmeyer?"

"Yes sir, I am. And who might you be?"

"I am Doctor Joseph Rothert. I wish to speak with you and your son."

"Doctor, you are in the right place. I was informed only minutes ago of your visit." James was yet to invite Joseph inside from the chilly autumn breeze.

"Mr. Wehmeyer, your son, August, was a patient of mine and my daughters at the Battle of Langensalza before we were shipped to Bohemia. He was influential in the short life of our pastor's son, Otto Braun. My daughter is a Red Cross nurse. She and your son have stayed in contact via mail for the last two months. May I come in and speak with you and your wife?"

James was embarrassed. "Oh yes, of course, I am so sorry, where are my manners? Please come inside." Walking to the dining room, James felt he must ask. "Your daughter is the one sending my son those letters. He has kept the identity of the author from us, only his twin sister knows. Please sir, join us for coffee and I believe we have a piece of apple pie still available." James led Joseph to the table. August faintly overheard the conversation.

As the footsteps came closer, August rose from his chair, extended his hand, and spoke. "Dr. Rothert, sir, it is an honor to have you in our home. My sister, just this afternoon, read Maria's most recent letter to me. It said you would visit us with a proposal. I did not expect…"

"Son, I am sorry to interrupt your family dinner, but I was called back to Cologne unexpectedly. My mother has taken a turn for the worse. I give you my apologies." Joseph was always gracious, and August felt his concern for his mother from the intonation in his voice.

"Please, sir, have a seat. I will retrieve my wife with coffee and pie. You two may discuss the purpose for your visit until we return." Dr. Rothert touched August gently. "How is the shoulder? Any infection? Are you regaining your strength?"

"Better every day, sir." August called to his father on his way to the kitchen. "Father, I wish to have Katarina join us in this discussion, but no one else, just Mother, you, and her." James turned to give Joseph an inquisitive glance.

Within a few minutes, the parties settled around the table. James spoke first. "For some reason, I do not feel this is a social call, Doctor. You met my son for one day, and your daughter and my son have been writing ever since. It seems peculiar. Is anything wrong?"

"I agree sir, they became friends immediately after our encounter with Otto. I am here because I am a professor of surgery at Chiate, and Von Bismarck is sending me to Boston to study new surgical techniques."

"That is impressive, but why are you here? What do we have to do with your career, not to mention Von Bismarck?" Ida and James looked at each other with consternation.

"My daughter and your son have become close via the written word, and she was around him for less than forty-eight hours. To be blunt, your son knows not what she looks like; he only knows her, and her him, by their letters. And she witnessed his heroism. I liked him from the beginning." Joseph hesitated while the foreheads of both Ida and James wrinkled."

"Go on, Doctor."

"I am here to ask if you would allow August, with his permission of course, to travel with me and my daughter to Boston for three months. There are new techniques for removing foreign bodies from the eyes, such as splinters and shrapnel. I want to offer your son an opportunity to regain his vision. By doing nothing, your son will be blind the remainder of his life." The Wehmeyer family listened intensely. "I examined his eyes within hours of his wound, but there was nothing I could do; I did not have the skills. Anything I attempted would have caused more damage and probable infection. This new technic may, and I say the word 'may' emphatically, allow August to regain his sight. Once again, I cannot impress upon you enough, this surgery is experimental. The worst which could happen is he remains blind."

The conversation continued and August remained silent. The trip would cost the Wehmeyers nothing. It would be funded by the Prussian government. "I am unsure," said Ida, "he has been through so much and his father believes he can regain his pottery skills without his sight."

"I have my doubts as well," said James. "I have little faith in modern medicine."

"Well, I just thought I would present…"

August interrupted. "I will go, sir, but only if you promise Maria goes with us." Katarina squeezed August's hand under the table. He turned his face in her direction, "Katerina, I cannot be alone and without you for three months in the darkness. I need Maria to help me handle my fears and recovery until I return home. If it works, I will see her face. Sir, is your daughter as beautiful as she is sweet in her letters?"

"Even more so, young man, she will give you a reason to live as she has me. I have never seen her more excited than when your letters arrived. Your bravery and your letters helped her through a mentally traumatic time. She shared a few of them with her mother and me. The respectful and romantic style by which you communicate has helped her recovery. You are quite a writer, son."

August was baffled. The letters he dictated to Katerina seemed plain and factual. Katarina gave a subtle smile unnoticed by all. She wrote what August told her, but added lines she knew every woman, including herself, wanted to hear. "My brother is tough on the outside, but what a lovely, elegant heart he possesses." She squeezed his hand even harder with a smile on her face. He understood. August smiled back.

Joseph was shown out the door. Hilda and Katarina cried for varied reasons. James and August said nothing. In two short months, August, Maria, and Joseph docked in Boston Harbor.

20

A Day of Decision For So Many

Boston City Hospital
December 17, 1866

Snow fell gently on the New England town of Boston as the sounds of Christmas filled the air. The jingling of bells on the horse-drawn sleighs sprinkled the streets with holiday joy. August's sense of smell, his hearing, and his touch heightened after spending six months in darkness. But the heady odor of bleach irritated his nostrils as he lied quietly in his room of the Boston City Hospital. Most wards housed a dozen patients, but due to the experimental nature of his surgery and the status of Dr. Joseph Rothert, August was alone.

The two weeks since August's surgery were brutal, fueled by his last vision of the hill outside of Langensalza. Except for the obscure sounds of pain floating down the hallway, or indistinguishable conversations outside his room, August was submerged in the secluded vacuum of his mind. So, he lived for those moments of bliss when he heard Maria's voice and smelled the sweet scent of her perfume. The soft touch of her hands and her gentle kisses on his forehead were euphoric. Maria shared with him what she learned from attending lectures at Harvard with her father. August was fascinated by her new knowledge of medicine. But today would be different. August's bandages would be removed; the success or failure of his surgery would be determined.

Shortly after breakfast, Joseph and Maria entered August's room with the surgeon. Maria's heart pounded like a hammer on a blacksmith's anvil. August was calm. Joseph began the conversation. "August, Dr. Murphy will remove your bandages. When he does, keep your eyelids shut until he tells you to open them. And when you do, open them slowly. Do you understand?"

"Yes sir, I understand." The bandages were unwrapped; the gauze pads were peeled from his eyes.

"August, open your eyes slowly and look at my fingers." His eyelids fluttered as the first rays of light in months pierced his pupils. "Well son, what do you see?"

"The blur is slightly better. I can see colors, but they are faint. I see no detail." The room was silent.

"Do you feel pain?"

"I did when I first opened my eyes, but it is waning." August's voice remained tranquil. He harbored no hope from the beginning; quiet tears ran down Maria's face. Joseph gripped her hand and placed his finger on her lips.

"I am sorry, son, but I had my doubts. The splinters went deep into your iris causing your pupils to remain open. That is why you only see a blur. Your pupils are damaged and incapable of dilating. In other words, you will never be able to focus.

"Not sure I understand, Doctor."

"What I am saying is, your sight will always be blurred unless we discover a technic to repair your iris. As of now, we have no way to do that." Dr. Murphy was surprised at August's tranquility and what appeared to be an immediate acceptance of his situation.

"What now?"

"I must declare you legally blind. You will need to wear dark glasses in bright light; normal glasses will be of no help. You will be unable to read. You will see shadows, maybe some dull colors." Dr. Murphy said all he needed to say. The surgery was a failure.

Maria approached August. She clutched his hand and stroked his hair. Joseph spoke. "August, I am sorry if I gave you any false hope, but we all knew, including you, this was experimental. Son, again you amaze me with your bravery and courage, especially now that you know your future will be challenged. I will begin preparations to send you and Maria back to Prussia."

"I thank all of you for your kind and competent treatment. I am a victim of war. I enlisted. It was my choice to fight for my country. None of you must feel any sympathy for me. You all did your best. But now, I must contemplate my future." August sighed. "Sir, I thank the Lord I was able to spend precious time with your daughter. It will be the highlight of my life. I never felt this way about anyone, and I never will again. Maria, I will miss you."

Maria looked at her father, then at Dr. Murphy. "Can we have a moment, gentlemen?" The room cleared.

Maria turned with a scowl unseen by August, but he heard in her voice. "Did you just tell me goodbye, August Wehmeyer? How dare you, soldier boy. Do you really think you can get rid of me that easily? You have been in my head every day since I found you with a musket ball through his shoulder and blood running from your eyeballs. I dumped a Hanoverian boy in a patch of thorn bushes to get back to you and Otto. Then I saw you digging underneath him with your fingernails. To impress me even further, you made me tie you to a wagon so you could stumble blindly back to camp and protect my best friend. Say auf wiedersehen one more time, and I will bop you on the head with this bed pan. I am here to stay."

August could do nothing but stare through his bloodshot eyes at the indistinct figure of Maria. "No, my dear, I must say good-bye. I refuse to do this to you. I can tell you want to study medicine and become a doctor someday. I will be blind and illiterate from here on. The only skill I possess is throwing pottery. I refuse to return to Berlin and be disabled August Wehmeyer, the boss's blind son, pitied by all his friends for the rest of his life. I would love nothing more than to have a career and family of my own someday, but who wants a blind man for their spouse?"

"If you will not return, I will stay here with you."

"I will miss you terribly. I love you, Maria Rother, but I understand."

"August, did you not hear what I said? You're blind, not deaf. I said let us stay here together."

"'Let us stay where, Maria? Do you mean you and I stay in America? That's crazy. Why would you ever do that when you have a prominent family and a wonderful future in Prussia? You need to think this through. What you are feeling is pity. Do not pity me, Maria."

"I love you, August Wehmeyer. I mean it. I am leaving the room and speak to Father." Maria left to find him and express her desire. August was convinced Joseph would talk sense into his daughter.

Joseph stood in the hallway with Dr. Murphy. "Is he alright, Maria. The shock must be terrible for that young man. Perhaps when he returns to Prussia and joins his family, he will find acceptance within himself. It will not be easy for any of them."

"Father, he does not wish to return. He says he does not want to be pitied by his friends and family."

"But what is his choice. He cannot stay here by himself. Who will take care of him? He has no money, and his career opportunities are severely limited."

"I will, Father. I will stay here with him. I just started at the University in Cologne. Why can I not attend a university here? I speak fluent English."

Dr. Murphy saw this was a family matter and dismissed himself. Joseph did not look at Maria. He stared blankly over her head; he was

129

silent as he delved into the depths of his intellect. "I have considered you attending an American university, but August was not part of the equation. Do you understand the commitment you must make to care and support a blind man? This sounds like a quick decision."

"So was joining the Red Cross, but it turned out fine."

"You were almost shot, and you were nearly hanged."

"But I wasn't. Tell me more about what you have considered."

"You remain here and attend Harvard for your undergraduate degree. I spoke with Von Bismarck, and he has already approved your scholarship due to your service to Prussia in the war. It is a unique opportunity for you to study abroad."

"But that does not solve the problem of August. Von Bismarck would not approve of supporting him financially. What would we do for money?"

"Exactly my point, Maria. I ask again; are you sure you want to take this responsibility?"

"Yes, now go on. How do we solve the problem of money? You must have ideas, you always do."

"Well, the Prussians and Americans are establishing a foreign exchange program to send medical students back and forth to be trained in each other's new surgical technics."

"Excellent."

"August's surgery was a convenient coincidence to my trip. My mission in America was not only to learn new technics, but to find a place to house Prussian students. In other words, set up a dormitory. Our students and the Americans would have a place to gather and share their knowledge and cultures. King Wilhelm feels our two countries will be powerful allies someday."

Maria smiled. "Tell me more, Father."

"A large mansion has been purchased by our government. You and August could maintain the premises, be the custodians. He could learn braille. He may not be able to see, but he will be able to read. I see many creative opportunities. But I must ask, what is your personal relationship with August? Do you want it to be more than friends?"

Maria ignored the question. "Father, all is fine while I am a student, but what happens when I graduate? Can we remain in the dormitory?"

"I have contemplated you teaching wartime medicine and trauma care at Harvard as you continue with your post-graduate studies."

"Why would their medical school need that? There is no war and no American Red Cross, only the one in Europe.

"People in the U.S. government are aware of the Geneva Convention, but when the Civil War ended, no one pursued it. There is an interesting woman lecturing through the Northeast and Midwest. Her name is Clara Barton. I believe we should take the time to meet with her."

"What experience does she have in warfare medicine?"

"More than you, my dear, almost more than me. I met her in 1864 at Fredericksburg when the Union Army was advancing on Richmond. On her own, she setup a hospital and logistic center as the wounded poured in."

"So, the United States has a form of Red Cross?"

"No, the International Red Cross was not established until 1864. Miss Barton was probably unaware of its existence. She treated the wounded with no training, and unofficially raised money for supplies and surgeons. I worked with her at Fredericksburg, just as you and I did at Langensalza. You two have a lot in common."

"She sounds incredible. I would love to learn from her. But what is her goal now that America is at peace?"

"I am told she is forming an organization not only to support soldiers, but also natural disasters like hurricanes, forest fires, and tornadoes. All those events need triage and treatment. I will make arrangements for us to meet."

"Well, let me share all this with August. I love you, Father."

Maria returned to August's room and spoke without hesitation, "I talked to Father; he has a plan."

"He is going to tie you up, put you in a crate, and ship you back to Prussia. I knew he would be the voice of reason." In his heart, August wanted to be wrong.

'No, silly man." Maria revealed her father's ideas and the living arrangements in the dormitory, how it would be large enough for them to have individual quarters.

"What do I do for money, Maria? I must pay rent, and I must eat."

"Room and board will be free for us, and we will receive a stipend for being custodians."

"I would become a custodian? I would change sheets and clean toilets?"

"Wait, August, there is more. Since I speak English, and only one of a few nurses in the world trained for a battlefield, Harvard will pay me to teach a nursing class in trauma care." Maria was getting more excited with every word she spoke.

"Maria, I refuse to be a stumbling blind man making beds and cleaning toilets for the rest of my life." He was disheartened.

"What do you want to do, August? Certainly, you realize you have serious limitations."

Reality smacked August in the face, like those splinters on the hillside. "Maria, before I left Berlin, my father took me to his pottery kilns where I attempted to throw earthenware as I did before the war. Even with bandages on my eyes, I felt the faultlessness of the clay in my hands. The other potters were amazed by my skills. Maria, for room and board, I will maintain the dormitory; it is a more than generous offer. But I want to be a potter. I want to caress the clay in the palms of my hands. My lack of sight has enhanced my sense of touch and intensified my inner vision of what I can create.

Maria was excited. "Oh August, less than an hour your hopes of a normal life were shattered, but you always find new ways to be my

The Great Great Aunts from Prussia

hero. What do you think? Is that a yes? Can we stay here together?" Maria kissed him on the lips for the first time. "I love you, my warrior."

"Maria, I must speak with your father before I agree. Ask him to come in, please." Maria retrieved her father who waited in the hallway.

"August, I assume my daughter told you of my proposal. Are you agreeable?" Joseph was stoic; he had his reservations.

"Sir, your offer is most generous, and I will maintain the dormitory, but I want to be more than a custodian someday. My goal is to hone my skills and produce breath-taking, artistic pottery. In my youth, I found the pottery of ancient cultures my passion; it still is. I accept your offer as long as you are aware of my ultimate goal."

"I respect your ambitions, son. I would have expected nothing less. With our contacts here, I am confident we can find you employment in the manufacturing district."

'Sir, I have only one remaining question."

"Yes son, what is it?" Maria feared the next question may end the fairy tale.

"If she will have me, may I have your daughter's hand in marriage?" August grew anxious since he was unable to see their facial responses.

Joseph looked at Maria; her face beamed as she nodded her head up and down. "Yes, you may, and with my deepest blessing."

"Maria, will you marry me?"

"Yes, soldier boy." Maria kissed August passionately.

Within thirty days, Maria and August were married. Joseph never imagined he would give his daughter's hand to a blind Prussian soldier in the city of Boston. Then again, he never imagined his daughter would be the first Red Cross nurse on a battlefield. They prepared their new home for Prussian students. Maria taught August English and braille. Joseph sailed back to Prussia with a stack of letters and a briefcase of wedding photographs. Within a year, Maria gave birth to a son, the first of eight children. They named him Otto.

"Well, my precious, that is the story of how my mother and father met and got married. Did you like it?"

"Hold on, Aunt Carrie. You still haven't told me how your father got famous. You can't stop now."

Carrie smiled. She knew how to keep her little nephew interested; she would tease his curiosity. "Okay, I will tell you and when I am done, I will give you a very special present. I am sure you will love it."

21

The Home of the Wehmeyer Family
Successful and Loving

BOSTON, MASSACHUSETTS
1867

Snow blew sideways as the blustering winds of winter swept through the streets of Boston. A constant flow of Prussian medical students arrived at the dormitory. Bestowed upon these brilliant students were the most charming of accommodations, maintained by the gracious new Wehmeyer family. To everyone's pleasant surprise, the arrival of August and Maria's first child coincided with the couple's first anniversary of marriage. In her adolescent days, Maria spoke often of her desire to have a large family. So, upon the revelation of the coming child, Von Bismarck showed his respect for Joseph and Maria by approving the construction of a new wing to the mansion. The family needed privacy, and the students needed silence. With more children expected, the new wing worked well for all.

Maria attended classes, as well as taught English and trauma medicine. August was given a job as a potter at a well-respected factory in the manufacturing district of Boston. But quickly, the company was surprised and very pleased with this blind man's proficiency of commercial vases and fruit bowls. And then they were awestruck by his ability to create elegant and expensive décor for the rich. His reputation spread. Some of his works were sent back to Prussia and presented to King Wilhelm as a thank you gift from the Rotherts. The pieces were displayed in many Prussian palaces.

As the years passed, August's fame continued to grow. He possessed the unique skill to create any shape from a piece of raw clay. He was no longer known as just a potter; he was now considered an artistic sculptor. And although he was unable to decorate his work himself, he was in high demand from artists who decorated his works to perfection. His partnership with artists spread, not only throughout Boston, but throughout New England and Midwest America. August's workload increased, causing his royalties to increase. And as the royalties increased, the Wehmeyer family became financially comfortable. Maria was proud.

In the fall of 1880, James Longworth came to his wheel. August felt a firm hand squeeze his shoulder. A familiar voice, one heard before but never directed at him, stood over him. August was concerned. He thought, *my artisanship, if not artistic prowess, is above reproach. Possibly the company is being sold or they are cutting back on employees.*

"August, I am Mr. Longworth."

"Yes sir, I recognize your voice. How may I help you?"

"I wish to meet with you in my office. We must chat. Take my arm and come with me, please."

"Mr. Longworth, I hope there is no problem, sir. It appears from your sales my work is in demand; artists seem most pleased with my designs. I love creating their requested textures and designs for their visions. I only regret that I cannot see their finished pieces. They must be beautiful." August could not see Mr. Longworth's smile, but it was one which applauded August's competence, as well as his humility. He felt the passion in August's voice.

"No, no, August. Nothing is wrong, nothing at all. Please join me."

The Great Great Aunts from Prussia

August held the owner's forearm and followed him up a flight of steps. He heard a door close behind them. He was seated in a comfortable leather chair; its odor was strong and pleasing. He heard Mr. Longworth sit in the chair beside him.

"I have an interesting proposition for you, August, and I do not need an answer right away. I am aware of your dedication to your wife and family, and them to you."

"Thank you, sir. My family, all of them, are most supportive of me." August was smiling. He sensed the conversation was moving in a positive direction.

"August, few men blinded in battle can rise to your success level as an artist, a husband, and a father. You are a true hero and an inspiration to many." August blushed, but he knew he was not in Mr. Longworth's office just to receive compliments. This is a business. "I understand you have a wife and six children but hear me out." Mr. Longworth's voice sounded enthusiastic.

August was puzzled. "Yes sir, I'm listening." August looked through his dark glasses at the blur of his boss beside him.

"August, my sister-in law, Maria Longworth, lives in Cincinnati, Ohio. Together we are opening a factory called Rookwood Pottery."

"Congratulations, sir. Not sure where Cincinnati is, but I assume it is a nice city if your brother and his wife live there." August did not know what else to say.

"My brother died of tuberculosis last year, and I wish to help his widow and her family support themselves." Mr. Longworth stared at the wall, sadly reminded of his brother's passing. "My brother was wealthy and well-known, not only in Cincinnati, but internationally."

"I am sorry, sir, but how does all this involve me." August went silent.

"Rookwood Pottery will be more than a pottery factory. It will be much more. Allow me to explain. The Longworth family in the Midwest is prominent in the art circles of that region. My sister-in-law and I are funding the construction of state-of-the-art kilns and bringing artists from all over the world into Cincinnati. Our goal is to produce the most well-known pottery of all time."

"Okay, sir, but again, what does this have to do with me? My family is here."

"My sister-in-law has recruited some of the most prodigious artists in the world and they support her venture. They paint beautifully, but they are not sculptors. You are, by far, the most incredible clay sculptor I have ever seen in all my years of production. You are on the level of the classics. So, I told her about you."

"Thank you, sir, but please share your proposition with me."

"August, would you consider moving to Cincinnati with your family and working for Rookwood Pottery?" He was sure he knew the answer to the relocation but needed to start the negotiation.

"Mr. Longworth, the day I proposed to my wife, I told her and her father my ultimate goal was to create classic works of art. I can still see those ancient pieces in the Berlin Museum of Art. I would love to accept your offer...."

"August, I did not expect a yes so quickly. I am pleasantly stunned."

"No, sir, you did not allow me to finish." Although August could not see his boss's reaction, he sensed it. "I cannot do that to my family. My wife loves teaching, and the intellectual stimulation from our students in the dorm is not only part of her life, but the lives of our children. I am sorry, sir." August's career already surpassed his dreams, but a geographical move would be selfish and disruptive to his entire family.

"August, I expected an overall rejection, but what if we compromise? I can arrange for an escort to travel with you to Cincinnati and back, let's say, three months there, three months here. Would you consider that? I promise you a sizeable raise along with contractual royalties from the artists. It will be quite lucrative."

August was given an opportunity to achieve his dream and bring pride to the hearts of Maria and his children. "Sir, I will give you my answer tomorrow. I must discuss this with my wife and children." August was flooded with the same excitement he felt when Maria said she would marry him.

"Of course, but this project will find its way to the pinnacle of the artistic history of pottery. Rookwood Pottery will be famous worldwide. There will be wings of museums dedicated to it someday. Think it over carefully." August was led back to his workstation. As he sat, his grin was so strong his cheeks began to cramp.

"So, he went to Cincinnati? Is that how he got famous? And that is how you and Aunt Mayme got here?"

"Yes, he took the job and traveled back and forth for years. Mayme and I were in our early teens when the whole family moved here permanently."

"Where is Aunt Mayme? I haven't seen her in a few days. Is she sick?"

"She hasn't felt well lately, but she will be fine. Wait here, Alex." Carrie went to the China cabinet and returned with a beautiful vase. "There you are, my precious. A gift for you from your Aunt Mayme and me."

"Your father made this? It is really cool. And it looks really old."

"Take good care of it. It is one of the few pieces not in a museum."

Alex got up and gave Carrie a big hug. "Thank you, I will keep it forever."

"Well Alex, that is the story. Your mother said this is the last day she needs to work for her friend, so we will not see you every day. It has been fun telling you the Wehmeyer story. Hope to see you soon. Let's get some cookies and milk before your mother arrives."

"Deal."

22

Mayme's Begins her Slide Down a Dark Path

Cincinnati, Ohio
November 1956

The phone rang at the Randell household. "Mary, this is Carrie. I am calling from Dr. Ventress' office. I tried earlier but could not reach you. I had to call your mother. She picked up Art from work and they came to my house right away. I need your help." Carrie's voice was shaking; something was wrong.

"Carrie, are you okay? What is happening?"

"I am fine. It is Mayme." Mary was not surprised after observing Mayme's recent behavior.

"Did she have a stroke or heart attack? Why did you call Mom and Dad instead of the Life Squad?"

"Mayme is here with me, so is Art and Ethel."

"Okay Carrie, tell me what happened." Mary's panic was subsiding, but not her curiosity.

"Mayme got up this morning and on her way to the bathroom, I heard a dining room chair crash to the floor. I shuffled as fast as I could to see what happened. Mayme was lying on the floor."

"Oh no, she fell? Is she all right? Did she break anything?" Mary deduced it might have something to do with her morning sambuca nips.

"We don't think so."

"So, no need for an ambulance?"

"I wanted to call one just in case, but the stubborn old bat wouldn't let me. She said it would wake the neighbors, but that wasn't the reason; I know my sister. She did not want those handsome men to see her in her bra and panties, and with no teeth." Mary laughed under her breath, but she heard frustration in Carrie's voice. "I helped her back to bed. She is like lifting a sack of potatoes. Art and Ethel came over as fast as they could. Ethel and I tried to dress her, but she couldn't decide what to wear. 'Which hat should I wear, this red one or my blue bonnet? I think my flowered dress would go better with the blue bonnet.' When she finally decided, she was like a rag doll. I almost went for a nip of her Sambuca myself, but it was empty."

"Carrie, that is so Mayme and it sounds sort of funny." Carrie ignored the comment.

"Art helped her down the steps to his car. He is a strong man, your father. He could have carried her all the way if need be. She insisted we go to Dr. V's first, not the hospital. Dr. V just now made the decision to call the ambulance. He wants her in the hospital for a few days to run some tests."

"So, how is she now?"

"She looks terrible; she is white as a ghost. Her fingernails are purple and she is panting like a dog. This is not good." Since summertime, Carrie watched Mayme's downhill spiral gaining momentum.

"Does the doctor think it was a stroke?"

"He thinks it is pleurisy from her heavier than normal drinking. And the drinking does not help her confusion and forgetfulness. Francis would have turned seventy this year. She is not handling it well at all."

"Carrie, who is Francis?" Mary had never heard the name before now.

"Oh Mary, forget I ever said that, please, and don't ever ask Mayme, ever, ever, ever. Never say his name aloud." Mary's eyes widened. "Can you cover for me while I go to the hospital?" Carrie then remembered, "Oh dear, what time must you pick up Alex from school?"

"He gets out at 3:15, so I must leave at three."

"Dr. V will be fine with that. We are all family to him." Carrie worked for the elderly doctor for years and was proud to be a nurse like her mother.

As always, Mary coordinated the plan. She would meticulously remind everyone of their duties. She was the planner for the family since age twelve. She raised her very young brother and sister due to her mother's alcoholism. She was still everyone's mother.

Unexpectedly, Carrie began to whimper into the phone. She whispered, "Mary, I need you."

"I know, Carrie, I have it under control. I will be there in …"

Carrie interrupted. "No, Mary, I need you in a different way. I must share something with you which may prevent someone from getting hurt." Mary assumed it was Mayme with her alcohol problem and her rapid onslaught of Alzheimer's. But Carrie harbored a secret which was the cause of Mayme's malaise, not the effect. Carrie continued to whisper, "What I will tell you must not be shared with anyone in the family, not your husband, Art, or Ethel. Promise me, only you can know."

Mary was silent for a moment. "Carrie, why me? Why am I the only one entrusted with your secret?"

"I must tell someone, or I will burst. Along with Dr. V., you and I may be the only ones able to help Mayme. I love our family, and because I do, you must not share until she and I both have passed. Please honey, I need you."

"Carrie, what night this week would be good for you?"

"No, it must be tonight while Mayme's not home. I do not want her to suspect anyone other than her and I know this story. She would never forgive me, and it would make things worse. It must be tonight."

Mary went from curiosity to deep concern. "Tonight, it is. Once I get the family feed and settled, I will pick you up at the hospital. Call me when you are ready. I will bring dinner. Do you want Blackberry wine?"

"Mary, I love you, my sweet little niece, but no wine tonight."

"I love you too, Carrie."

The phone call ended.

Mary picked Carrie up from the hospital. Mayme was in twilight from the medication she was given to ease the pain of her bruised hip.

Mary brought meatloaf, mashed potatoes, and green beans. They talked about the storytelling days last summer when Alex learned about his ancestry. "Carrie, it was fun listening to Alex at the dinner table attempting to tell us about your mother and father. He still doesn't get the Russia/Prussia thing, but he loves the vase you gave him. Do you think you can write some notes for him so he will remember it when he gets older?"

"I jotted notes each night and I have a few photographs. He was so attentive. He is a smart kid. We had fun last summer."

They cleared the table and retired to the living room. Carrie kissed Mary on the cheek. "Are you ready, honey? I will begin where I left off with Alex. I must warn you; this story is not pleasant. It will cause you to see Mayme and I in a different light. You may not like me anymore, but I must tell somebody. Since Mayme and I are the only ones left alive from my immediate family, you will be the only person to carry this story forward, but only after we are gone. Perhaps someday that little boy of yours will write the entire story, including the ending. It may be of some value for future generations to understand the life-long relationship between Mayme and me."

"I am ready."

"You know my father worked in Boston half the time, and Cincinnati half the time."

"Yes, he was a famous potter and sculptor at Rookwood Pottery."

"But what you do not know is why the entire family left Boston. My mother was a well-respected professor at Harvard. Let me begin there."

Mary thought, *what am I about to discover about my two great-aunts from Prussia?*

23

Boston to Cincinnati
The Family Separation is Bittersweet

September 1888

Dear my beloved August,

All is well on the home front. The three months we spend apart seem much longer than the three we spend together. Otto moved into the dorm at Boston College last week. I wish you could have been here to experience his excitement. It is good for him to leave home, but I was in tears as I watched him pack his clothing. He insisted on taking some of your pottery with him to decorate his room. All of us are so proud of you. Someday I pray we can visit you in Cincinnati. It would be such an educational trip for the children as well as myself.

The rest of the children are exceptional as well. The older four have been quite helpful to Mrs. Schmidt and me taking care of the students. They learn so much from discussions with the Prussians, although some wish to be referred to as Germans these days. Mayme and Carrie, at nine and eight, are too young to care about conversation, and they do not cheerfully accept any domestic responsibilities. Then there is

Francis. At three, he is still the highest of maintenance. It is all I can do to keep up with the little chipmunk. He is a mischievous one. But he has my heart; all he needs to do is smile.

We all love it when your letters arrive, but not nearly as much as when you walk in the front door. The house seems incomplete without you, my love. Please make time accelerate until you return.

I so look forward to the beginning of our holiday season when you return in October.

Write soon and often, my hero,
Maria

24

The Day Heaven Crashes upon the Wehmeyer Family

Boston
February 14, 1889

Holding hands, Mayme and Carrie skipped joyfully home; the boxes containing letters from their school sponsored, 'Friendship Day,' stuffed into their backpacks. They entered the house, and without hesitation, scampered up the stairway to their bedroom. The reading of their friends well wishes would be fun, but the hope of a fledgling love letter caused them to bubble inside. As they threw their winter coats and warm mittens on the floor, they heard their mother calling from the vestibule. "Mayme, come down here please? I need your help, honey."

The sisters peered at one another, their body language exuded disappointment. They could not wait another second to read their letters with the anticipation of one from a little boy whose fancies they would cherish forever. "Yes Mother, we will be right down," Mayme murmured with discontent. They moved slowly down the curved staircase. Maria stood at the bottom with four-year-old Francis who held his mother's hand.

"Mayme, since you are the oldest, I must give you this responsibility. Carrie, you may go back to your room." Carrie smiled but remained by Mayme's side. They were inseparable.

"What is it, Mother?"

"Mrs. Schmidt's son is sick with a fever, and he stayed home from school today."

"I am sorry to hear that, Mother, but what does that have to do with me?" Mayme could not have been less interested. Her mind was fixated on her letters.

"What that means, Mayme, is I must run to the market myself to gather dinner and breakfast supplies for the students. Your siblings are doing their homework in the library now so they may help me prepare dinner. They must not be distracted."

"So again, what do you need from me? I have homework as well. I have an important exam tomorrow." Maria knew it was Friendship Day. It was something her older children had celebrated.

"Mayme, I will be back shortly. You must watch Francis until I return home. Play with him or read him a fairy tale." Maria gave Francis' hand to Mayme.

"Aww Mother, why can't you take him with you? I told you, I have..."

Maria interrupted Mayme, perturbed with her daughter's attitude. "Mayme Wehmeyer, you can study while the others are helping me with dinner. Now, no more objections. Watch your brother." With that, Maria put on her coat, her woolen bonnet, and left the house.

"Read me a book, Mayme, come on, please. Read me the one about the witch who tries to eat the brother and sister, and they push her in the oven and burn her up. Come on Mayme, please. I'm gonna kill me a witch someday, I promise."

Mayme rolled her eyes. "Francis, you are such trouble compared to the rest of us. Take a nap; I will read to you when you wake up. Carrie and I have important schoolwork to do." The thought of those unread letters in their backpacks was unbearable.

"I'm not tired, Mayme. I just woke up from a nap, and I heard mother say you could do your schoolwork later. She did, I heard her. Come on, Mayme, play with me." Francis was so cute, and he learned how to use it to his advantage. The older children were possessed by their little sibling, but Mayme and Carrie were too close in age to see him as anything but competition, a sibling rival.

Suddenly, Carrie looked at Mayme. She had an idea. "Francis, let's play hide and seek. Mayme and I will go to our room, and you will go hide. Then we will try to find you. Doesn't that sound fun!" Mayme shook her head up and down with a huge grin, even though she did not quite get Carrie's scheme.

"Okay, Carrie, I like that game. Let's start in your room." Francis was ready to romp through the house and hide like a little monkey freed from its cage.

Carrie took Mayme's hand and climbed the stairs. Francis scurried up in front of them. He ran into his sisters' bedroom. Mayme stopped. "I don't get it Carrie. How will we read our letters if we are searching the house for the little urchin?"

"Mayme, we don't look for him. He will stay in his hiding place for a while, then, when he gets tired of not being found, he comes back."

"Then what?"

"We tell him he is such a good hider we couldn't find him. We tell him to hide again."

Carrie's idea now made sense; Mayme smiled. "Brilliant, Carrie." The girls went into their room. Francis was jumping on their bed. They let him until he got tired of it. He loved to do it because his mother never let him.

"Okay Francis, are you ready to go hide while we count to ten. Then we will come looking. Ready? Here we go: one, two, three…" Francis took off running.

Ten minutes later, Francis reentered the room, a heavy pout on his face. Letters were spread all over the floor. "You didn't look for me. I waited, but you didn't even look." Francis whined like every good little four-year old.

"Yes, we did. We looked everywhere, but you had such a great hiding place, we couldn't find you, so we gave up. You're a good hider, Francis." Mayme and Carrie giggled at the gullibility of their brother. "Okay, Francis, let's try it again." Carrie figured her mother would be home shortly and their chore would be over. They did it again, but Francis came back sooner, and Carrie used the same excuse.

"Okay Carrie, once more, but I won't make it as hard this time. I will give you a hint, the kitchen." Mayme and Carrie giggled at his innocence.

"Here we go: one, two, three…" Francis skedaddled, but before the girls could read another letter they heard the frightful sound of a crash, along with the simultaneous shattering of glass.

They looked at each other, their eyes widened. They raced down the stairway to the kitchen. At the end of the hallway, there it was. The ponderous oak China cabinet was laying on its face, the sound of Francis groaning beneath. He attempted to climb on top to hide. Francis's chest was crushed; his face and neck slashed by shattered glass.

"Oh Mayme, what do we do? He is pooling under his head and his eyes are rolled back in his head. He cannot breathe with that weight on him. Mayme, Mayme, what do we do?" Carrie was in a state of trepidation, unable to think or reason.

"Carrie, you grab that side, and I will get this side. Let's lift the cabinet off him." Both sisters lifted with all their strength, but Mayme's hand slipped, and her arm crashed through the glass door. The cabinet slammed onto Francis' chest once more. The broken glass slid down Mayme's forearm, slicing it like a tiger claw from her wrist to her elbow and severing her artery on its way. Blood pulsated from the slash. She dropped onto the floor, gripping the wound which was quickly draining the life from her body.

Suddenly, the front door opened. "Kids, I'm home." With that, Mayme crawled on her knees under the dining room table; she whimpered in pain. She was terrified as to what her mother would do to her when she saw Francis.

"Mayme, Carrie, Francis, are you upstairs?" Maria was escorted by two young boys from the market helping her home with the groceries. "Boys, go through the pantry and place the bags in the kitchen." But as they did, Maria heard one of the boys drop his groceries and scream, "Mrs. Wehmeyer, come quick! Hurry, hurry!"

Maria ran to the sight; Carrie was weeping hysterically. She then saw her precious son motionless under the China cabinet. She dropped to her knees and felt Francis's neck for a pulse. It was not there. "Boys, help me get this cabinet upright." When they did, Maria pulled a shard of glass from the back of Francis's bloody neck, but the blood only drizzled. Maria lifted his limp body in her arms and placed him on the dining room table. Blood ran from the corners of his mouth. She knew his lungs were crushed. Francis was dead.

"Mrs. Wehmeyer, what can we do? Please, what can we do?" The boys were aghast at the sight of so much blood and a dead child on the table in front of them.

"Carrie, where is Mayme? She was to watch him. She knows how he loves to climb." Maria grabbed Carrie firmly by the arm. "Where is she, young lady, where is she?"

"I don't know, Mother. I was upstairs in my room by myself when I heard the crash. I don't know where she is." Carrie was afraid of what her mother would do to her if she knew the truth, if she knew playing hide and seek was her idea. So, she lied, and it was a lie she would regret forever. It was a lie she would always know Mayme heard her tell.

Maria heard a heavy sob under the table. She saw a stream of blood coming out from the lacey tablecloth at her feet. She dropped to her knees. Mayme was covered in blood, shivering, whimpering, and hugging herself into a ball. Maria dragged her out. She saw the main artery on her forearm deeply sliced and knew it was critical.

"Mother, it is my fault. It is all my fault." Mayme was hysterical. "Don't save me. I don't want to live; I don't deserve to live. I want to die, Mother, I want to die right now! Francis is dead because of me. Let me die!"

"Hush child. **B**oys, I need you to take us back to camp before this soldier bleeds to death. Carrie, go outside and get in the wagon. I will need your help on the way back to camp." Maria ripped the tablecloth and tied a tourniquet around Mayme's arm. She found the strength to carry her to the street. But before she did, she put Mayme in a chair by the front door and returned to the dining room table. She removed one of Francis's shoes and put it at the top of his head.

As she did, one of the boys asked Maria, "Are you going to just leave your son on the table? Shouldn't we take him with us to the hospital, Mrs. Wehmeyer?" The boys and Carrie were confused. Mayme was losing consciousness.

"I learned from my father many years ago, we must leave those soldiers who will not survive so we can save the ones we can." Her voice was eerie. "Do not question me again, medic, do you understand? I am the head nurse here. You will do as I say, or I will have you court-martialed. We must get this soldier to Dr. Rothert's operatory immediately." The delivery boys were frightened. Mrs. Wehmeyer was no longer Mrs. Wehmeyer. She was not the sweet woman from the market. She was scary.

The boys helped Maria to the wagon with Mayme in her arms. She sat her upright. Carrie held her arm above her head as Marie tightened the tourniquet. "Go boys." They flicked the reins, and the horse began its hurried trot to the hospital. At the end of the first block, the driver whispered to the other boy, "She called us medics. We are just delivery boys, and Mrs. Wehmeyer is not crying at all. Where has her mind gone? Who is Dr. Rothert? And what is with the shoe?"

Mayme survived. Her arm was stitched and bandaged. She would carry the scar for the rest of her life. It would remind the entire family of the day Francis died. But for Mayme and Carrie, the scar would be far more than Francis's death. It would be a grueling reminder of their selfishness in wanting a boy, any boy, to care for them. Neither would ever marry. It would also be a reminder to Mayme that Carrie lied and put the blame completely on her. That emotional scar would remain deep, deep inside both forever and a confrontation would never be an option, only silence.

Within a year, Maria was unable to live with the memory of Francis' death in their Boston home. Another meal would never again be served in the dining room. August was unable to handle his grief in Cincinnati without Maria and his children. The family packed up and moved to Cincinnati within a year, where August was now an important part of the Rookwood Pottery legacy. However, he suffered from deep depression and died of grief at fifty-five. With most of the children nearly on their own, Maria Rothert Wehmeyer joined the American Red Cross working closely with Clara Barton and her fledgling organization. She taught nursing at the University of Cincinnati and wrote the early history of the International Red Cross in Europe. She served on the battlefield one last time in the Spanish American War of 1898. She died at age seventy-five. She saved many lives during her lifetime, but she was eternally haunted by her inability to save the three men she loved the most.

Carrie wept as she finished her account of her and her sister's tragic youth. Mary rocked her in her arms. "I am so sorry, Carrie. That is so sad. I will keep this to myself as you requested."

"Do you now hate me for what I did to Mayme?"

"Of course not, you were little girls."

"I want you to share this with Alex when Mayme and I are gone. Please, write the facts so he may write the story someday. He expressed a desire to do so, even though he is six. I have a strange premonition he will do it."

"Of course, so that is why Mayme seems troubled recently?"

Carrie did not respond. She pretended Mary was making a statement, not asking a question. She took a deep breath. There was more to the story, but she was unsure she wanted to tell it. To continue would taint her mother's honored and respected reputation.

25

Mayme Is Released from the Hospital Carrie Cries Out for Help

Cincinnati Ohio
November 1956

"Beckham residence, Alex speaking." Randall recently started his own business based out of their home and Mary helped. They trained Alex, now six-years-old, to answer the telephone in a professional manner and always with a smile on his face. Randal claimed people could hear a smile through the phone. It didn't make sense to Alex, but he did what he was told.

"Hello Alex, this is Aunt Carrie. May I speak with your mother, please?"

"Sure, Aunt Carrie, she is outside raking leaves. I just got home from school. I'll go get her." Alex hung up the telephone and ran to retrieve his mother. "Mom, Aunt Carrie is on the telephone, well, I mean, she was, but I accidentally hung up on her, sorry."

"Alex Beckham, you must be careful. What if it was a business call for your father, young man?" Mary was not happy with the mistake; the fact he was six did not seem to matter.

"Sorry Mom, really I am, but Aunt Carrie sounds out of breath." Alex stayed outside and threw his rubber ball against the garage doors. Mary rushed to call her back. She expected to hear of another health emergency.

Dialing the phone as fast as the rotor would recoil, her restless foot tapped on the hardwood floor. She lit a cigarette. After two rings, Carrie answered. "Carrie, I'm sorry Alex hung up on you. Are you okay?"

"I am fine, but Mayme is getting worse, honey." Carrie's voice quivered.

"What do you mean she is getting worse? I thought the medication was working and her lungs were clearing. She appeared much healthier when she returned from the hospital last week. I couldn't even tell she had been sick. It was the quickest recovery from pleurisy I've seen, especially at her age." Mary sensed something illogical, confusion wrinkling her brow.

"Mary, Mayme is fine for the moment. Let just say she is napping."

"What does 'let's just say she is napping' mean? Come on Carrie, out with it. You are hiding something. What is it?" Mary was now impatient.

"You know our secret about Francis, right? And you know how I let Mayme take the blame for his death when I lied to our mother?"

"Of course, how can I forget? You were a frightened little girl, Carrie, and Mayme decided to say nothing to protect her little sister. Please Carrie, get on with it."

"But I didn't tell you what happened after Francis's death."

"Yes, you did. You moved to Cincinnati, your mother taught nursing, then your parents died."

"There is more?"

"When we moved to Cincinnati, Mayme was never quite right." Carrie began to whimper.

"There you go again, Carrie. What do you mean 'not quite right'?"

"As I said, Mother and Father were devasted by the death of Francis, but what I didn't tell you is Mother insisted on having another child right away to replace Francis. But Father was so depressed he was totally against it."

"Did they? You have never spoken of that sibling either."

"Well, as always, Mother got her way. She was pregnant when we moved here; the child was born one year after Francis's death."

"Keep going."

"Mary, it was horrible. Mother perceived Mayme as tragically irresponsible. She blamed her, and her alone, for the death of Francis. So much so, she would never allow Mayme near the new baby. Even as the baby grew, Mayme was forbidden to be alone with him. She was not allowed to hold him, hug him, kiss him, nothing. Mother allowed me to babysit, but Mayme had to stay away. Mother showed her no forgiveness and no affection for the rest of her life." Carrie broke down in tears.

"Oh Carrie, that is dreadful. Mayme is so loving and caring to all of us, especially Alex." Suddenly, it made sense. "Oh, Carrie, do you mean…?"

"Yes dear, she loves her two nephews, Art and Alex. She loves them intensely because they are boys; to her they are Francis. Mother could keep Mayme away from our baby brother, but she did not have the power to keep her away from Art and Alex. Mayme needed to prove to all of us, but especially to herself, she was not the dangerous, horrible person our mother convinced her she was."

"So why didn't your older siblings support Mayme?"

"The older ones stayed in Boston to attend school. Only one sister came with us; that was Art's mother. None of our siblings blamed Mayme. In fact, Mother's actions drove a spike through the heart of the entire family forever."

"So, that is why you ended the story where you did with Alex. Now I understand."

"I was reluctant to tell you this part. I told Alex only about the heroic parts of our family. You now know the dark side, and the reason Mayme and I remained spinsters together all of our lives."

"Poor Mayme, my heart is breaking. And poor you, Carrie." Tears ran down Mary's face.

"Mary, I must tell you, Mayme made several attempts on her life over the years. Father put her in an asylum numerous times to protect her from herself. Mother did not care if she lived or died. That was another reason he died of grief so early. I promised Father on his death bed, I would care for her always; and I have. But it is getting worse, way worse." Carrie stopped.

"Oh Carrie, what do you mean?" Mary's heart began to race.

"Honey, her hospital stay was not for pleurisy. She thought, if she swallowed a whole bottle of aspirin along with a bottle of Sambuca, she would die in peace; but it didn't work. Dr. V gave her Ipecac to empty her stomach. That is why we took her there first. He said she was never in critical danger. But Art insisted she be admitted to observe her behavior. He knew she tried to kill herself over the years; he just never knew why." Mary went silent. "Mary, hello, are you still there?"

"What can I do, Carrie? Will she try again?"

"I don't know. But what I do know is she has finally turned her anger towards me."

"Has she threatened to hurt you?"

"Before now, she never wanted to hurt anyone, only herself. But she has become verbally cruel and abusive. This morning, she put my favorite dress in the toilet, sat down and peed on it. She giggled the whole time. It was maniacal."

"Mayme did that?"

"Yes, and she sticks her tongue out at me during dinner and throws food across the table. She acts like a little brat. And last night I opened my eyes to see her standing over me with her pillow; her smile was chilling and her laugh sinister."

"Oh Carrie, her behavior is escalating. She is overflowing with rage. She is out of control. She blames you for Francis's death, and why her mother disowned her."

"And she is right; I lied. Art calls her his 'Little Firecracker' and she behaves like a child around Alex, and I must say, they are adorable together. But she is at the breaking point. Between her dementia and out of control alcohol consumption, Art's Little Firecracker's fuse has been lit. Mary, I am frightened for her life and frightened for my own."

"Carrie, a while ago, you slipped and told me Francis would be seventy this year. Is that when it started?"

"Yes, I have never seen her drink this way. That is all she does; she drinks Sambuca and sleeps. She has passed out in her bed right now from drinking all morning. Could you come over before she wakes? I need you here. Maybe you will have some ideas about what I should do."

"Sure, but I must bring Alex. Randall won't be home until late. We can make dinner and talk?" Mary was concerned about Alex joining her.

"Oh Mary, my beautiful little niece, thank you."

"See you in an hour. Love you, Carrie."

"Love you too, Mary."

The call ended.

Mary parked in front of the Wehmeyer home; she turned off the motor. As Alex reached to open his car door, Mary grabbed his arm firmly. "Alex, before we go in you must promise me to do exactly what I say, no questions asked."

"Sure Mom, I always do what you say." Mary raised her brows and looked at Alex over top of her glasses. "Okay, I don't always, but I will this time." Alex was excited to visit his aunts. They treated him like a prince, and Mayme made him laugh.

"Alex, when we go into the house, stay behind me. Don't run for the living room, say hello, then dart for the cookie jar." Alex heard no playfulness in his mother's voice; something was wrong.

"Sure Mom, but why?"

"Alex, I said no questions. And if I tell you to run, you run to the car as fast as you can and lock yourself inside. This is important. Do you understand?"

"No Mom, I don't understand at all. Why do I have to stay behind you? Is there a robber or a wild animal or something in there? Maybe we should get Grandpa to help us. Dad left the baseball stuff in the trunk. Let's grab some bats." Alex was scared, not for himself, but for his mother.

"There are no robbers or wild animals inside, but I said no questions; I mean it. I will explain later." Mary squeezed Alex's arm tighter. He now knew she was really serious.

Mary and Alex walked up the steps to the front door. Mary rang the bell to announce her arrival. A face appeared at the storm door, then the inside door slammed so hard it shattered a pane of glass. Mary spun to protect Alex from the flying shards.

"Mom, that was Aunt Mayme, but it didn't look like Aunt Mayme." Mary reached for her spare key and unlocked the door. As they entered, Mary pushed Alex behind her with her arm. They crept to the living room like mice entering a lion's den.

After slamming the door, Mayme ran to the living room dressed only in her bra and panties, her floor length night gown flowed behind her. She was devoid of teeth. "Carrie, Carrie, it's Mother, she has returned from the market. She will be so angry when she finds out we were not watching Francis." Mayme ran to the dinette and hid under the table. Carrie cried; her face buried in her hands. Alex peeked out from behind his mother.

"Carrie, what is going on? Mayme slammed the door in our face and shattered one of the windowpanes."

"Mayme," Carrie called, "it is not Mother, it is Mary and Alex coming to visit. Everything is fine."

The Great Great Aunts from Prussia

Mayme called from under the table. "Carrie, you are just as responsible for Francis as I am. Hide and seek was your idea, not mine." Mayme painfully climbed to her feet. When she entered the living room, she stared at Alex. "There you are, you little stinker; you are okay. You were just fooling us by hiding under that cabinet. Sit down and don't move an inch while I help Mother with dinner." Alex was perplexed, and his Aunt Mayme looked creepy.

Mayme went to the kitchen and poured herself a full glass of Sambuca while Carrie wept on the sofa. Mary hugged her, rocking her like a child. Alex sat on the far end of the sofa as he was instructed. She leaned over and whispered into his ear, "Remember, if I say 'run,' run to the car like a jackrabbit; don't look back." Alex was old enough to realize this was not a game. But what was happening?

From the kitchen, Mayme saw Carrie and Mary in an embrace; she returned. "Wait a minute. You're not Mother, and you, little boy, are not Francis. Is this some sort of trick? I am supposed to be watching Francis, not you, whoever you are." Mayme was angry; Alex froze.

"Mayme, go back to the kitchen and leave us alone for a moment," said Mary. "Then I will help you make dinner." Mary attempted to bring Mayme back to the present, but it did not work.

"No Mother, you want me to leave the room because you think Francis is unsafe around me. You think I am a dangerous, irresponsible little girl, don't you Mother? You all think I am a terrible person, don't you? Well, I'm not." Haunting memories flooded her head. That gruesome day, years ago, became vivid. Mayme marched back to the kitchen then quickly returned, only this time with a butcher knife in hand. She grabbed Carries by the hair, pulled her head backward, and pointed the blade at her throat.

"Mayme, what are you doing?" Mary stared directly into her eyes; it momentarily paused the attack.

"This crybaby ruined my life. She was as much to blame as I was. But no, she blamed it all on me. 'I was up in my room by myself,' she told mother. I have had enough of you, Carrie. Instead of trying to kill myself this time, I am going to kill you, my wicked little sister. I am going to stab you through the chest like mother wanted to do to that Hanoverian, only I am going to do it." Mayme looked to the heavens and smiled. "You will forgive me when I tell you of Carrie's lies. Watch Mother, watch what I do to that precious little Carrie of yours."

"Mayme, not a day goes by I don't feel guilty about that lie. It is why I have never left your side, and it has not been easy. Go ahead, do it, do it Mayme. I cannot bear to watch you suffer any longer; spare me this agony." Carrie held her arms open.

But suddenly, Alex left the sofa and squeezed in between his aunts. "No Aunt Mayme, please don't hurt Aunt Carrie. I love you both. Please put the knife down, please!" Alex pleaded as tears ran down his cheeks.

Mary wanted to grab Alex but was afraid any quick movements would heighten Mayme's confusion and spawn an attack. But in that moment of silence, a look of serenity flushed Mayme's face as she looked at Alex. "Francis, is that you? I have not seen you in so many years, oh my little sunshine."

"No, Aunt Mayme, I'm your nephew Alex, but you always call me Art, remember?" Mayme struggled hard to put this ancestral puzzle together. "We go to the pool and splash and play dominoes. You used to give me horsey back rides to the park. Please don't hurt Aunt Carrie." Alex and Mayme locked eyes.

Mary stayed motionless. Mayme lowered the knife. She took Alex by the chin and lifted his face. "Mayme," said Mary, "look closely, it is Alex, not your Francis. Look into his face; You know him, you love him, and he loves you."

"I know who he is, and I would never hurt Art, I mean Alex." She kissed him on the forehead and gave him a gentle, toothless smile. She returned to the kitchen.

Mary grabbed Alex by the arm and pulled her close to her bosom. "Don't you ever do something like that again, Alex Beckham. I told you to stay behind me, did I not?"

"Mom, it is Aunt Mayme. She wouldn't hurt me. She is mad at Aunt Carrie for some reason. Who is Francis?"

They heard the butcher knife drop into the sink and saw Mayme leave the kitchen. She circled the rooms. They saw a faint object flow through the shadows. Mayme was headed to her bedroom. "She needs time to settle," said Mary. But it was not long before the three on the sofa received a gut-wrenching surprise.

Carrie rose to her feet; she was in a face-off with her sister. "Oh dear, Mayme, what are you doing? There is a little boy in the room. Get back in the bedroom right now, do you hear me, right now."

Shivers went through Alex's body, his eyes bulged. Mary did not know what was best, tell Alex to run, pull Carrie back on the sofa, or force Mayme back into the bedroom. Perhaps all three would be best.

In that moment of bewilderment, there she stood. Alex's Aunt Mayme, a woman in her seventies, stood stark naked in front of them. Gravity took its toll everywhere, but one area in particular. She bent at the waist and stared intensely into her sister's eyes. Then, with one side of her lip raised in disgust, she put her thumb to her nose, waggled her fingers, and in an evil raspy voice she grinded, "Kiss my ass, Carrie." Then, as quickly as she exposed herself, she strutted calmly back to the bedroom.

Carrie, once again, buried her face in her hands and sobbed uncontrollably. Mary held her head to her shoulder. "Alex, go to the bathroom and grab some tissues." But she quickly reversed her instruction. "No Alex, I am going to get Aunt Carrie some tissues so come with me." She reached the bathroom and watched to see if Mayme came back out. "Alex, get the tissue box, take it to Aunt Carrie, then run back as fast as you can. I must call your grandpa."

Before she made the call, she barricaded the bedroom door with a dining room chair under the knob, then she went to the music room to call Art.

"Hello" answered Ethel.

"Mom, is Dad there? I need to talk to him right away."

"Honey, can he call you back? I am making dinner, and he is napping.

"No, Mom. It can't wait. I mean, this is a real emergency. Wake him now. I do not have a lot of time." The panic was obvious in her daughter's voice.

"Is it Alex? Is he hurt? Why do you need your father?"

"No Mom, it is Mayme. Get him, no more questions." Mary was stern. Her mother knew not to mess with her daughter when she heard that tone.

"Art, Mary's on the phone, and says she needs to talk to you. It is an emergency involving Mayme." Ethel knew what was coming.

"Ethel, I told you never to wake me from my nap. It was a rough day in the factory. Did you tell her I...?"

"Art, she knows not to wake you, but she insisted, please Art. This must be really important." Art got up from the couch and shuffled to the telephone.

"This better be good, Ethel." Art picked the telephone off the stand. "Mary, I was napping. What do you want?" It was an ugly greeting.

"Dad, I need you here right now. Mayme flipped out and tried to stab Carrie with a butcher knife. Alex and I are here. I have her barricaded in the bedroom. You are the only one that can help us."

"I saw this coming. My little firecracker finally went off, did she? I will be there in fifteen. Keep her confined." Art hung up; he told Ethel to stay put. He put on his trousers and shirt and raced to the car.

Art joined the three of them in the living room. With Carrie sobbing on the sofa, and Alex totally befuddled, Mary relayed the events. Then Carrie described other disturbing behaviors from Mayme.

The Great Great Aunts from Prussia

Alex could no longer stay quiet, "And can someone please tell me, who is Francis? Aunt Mayme said she was looking for Francis when we came in, and then she called me Francis. Usually she thinks I am you, Grandpa."

"Alex, that's enough," Mary and Carrie glanced at each other. Alex needed to be quiet.

Art spoke, "Carrie, didn't you tell me you had a little brother who died of smallpox when he was very young?"

Carrie looked at Mary. "Yes Art, and Mayme loved our little brother very much. She was devastated, as we all were. That is why she adores all her nephews, you, and now Alex."

Art accepted the answer. "Mary, call Dr. Ventress and have him come tonight and sedate her. We must remove all alcohol from the house. Pour out the wine and Sambuca. Carrie, you keep beers in the fridge for me, right?"

"Always do, Art."

"Then Mary, let's get rid of those ourselves. Let's have some beers, daughter of mine."

"Mary, would you pour me a glass of blackberry wine, please?"

Alex looked at his mother. "Can I have some blackberry wine too, Mom? Aunt Mayme lets me drink it. She says it makes my tummy feel good, and it does. Then we laugh a lot." Alex had a smile on his face. All three glanced at each other and rolled their eyes.

Dr. Ventress came quickly. As they spoke, they heard the chair moving. Mayme was attempting to escape her confinement. Since it was a few hours since her last Sambuca, she was ready for an injection. She slept through the night. Carrie stayed with Ethel. Art slept on the couch protecting his loving Aunt Mayme from harm. The next morning, the decision was quick. Dr. V. admitted her to the State Mental Hospital and would arrange for a permanent commitment. In the early afternoon hours, a van arrived with men in white coats. Dr.

Ventress injected Mayme one last time before she was taken to the asylum. Art followed to help her settle into her new home.

Carrie, Mary, and Alex watched despondently from the porch; Carrie was in tears. Alex watched his mother embrace the brokenhearted sister. She wept for hours and slashed herself with guilt over and over. "Mary, this is all my fault. If I had not wanted to read those letters so badly, I would not have told Francis to go hide. He might still be alive. And if I had not let Mayme take all the blame, she would not have felt so unloved."

Alex watched quietly, but he could no longer hold back. "Aunt Carrie?"

"Yes, Alex."

"Who is Francis and when will you tell me that story?"

THE END